Functional Programming with JavaScript:

Simplifying Code with Modern Techniques for Better
Performance and Maintainability

Ethan B.Carter

TABLE OF CONTENT

Chapter 6
Advanced Functional Programming

6.1 Closures and Their Applications
6.2 Functional Composition with pipe() and compose()
6.3 Lazy Evaluation
6.4 Managing State with Functional Paradigms

Chapter 7
Performance Optimization

7.1 Functional Programming and Performance Trade-Offs
7.2 Memoization
7.3 Throttling and Debouncing

Chapter 8
Real-World Applications

8.1 Functional Patterns in React and Redux
8.2 Handling Asynchronous Data Streams with RxJS
8.3 Functional Programming in Back-End JavaScript
(Node.js)

Chapter 9
Best Practices and Tips

Chapter 1
Introduction to Functional Programming

Functional programming (FP) is a programming paradigm centered around building software by using pure functions, avoiding shared state, and leveraging immutability. It emphasizes declarative code, where the focus is on what to do rather than how to do it.

In JavaScript, functional programming has gained significant popularity due to its ability to create clean, maintainable, and reusable code. FP is especially effective in managing complex data transformations and handling side effects predictably.

Key Benefits of Functional Programming

Improved Readability: Pure functions and declarative code make understanding logic simpler.
Easier Debugging: Without shared state, functions are easier to test and debug.
Reusability: Functions written in FP are modular and reusable across different parts of an application.

Concurrency-Friendly: Immutability helps avoid conflicts in multi-threaded or asynchronous environments.

By combining functional programming concepts with JavaScript's modern features like arrow functions, higher-order functions, and ES6+ syntax, developers can write performant and maintainable code for both front-end and back-end applications.

1.1 What is Functional Programming?

Functional Programming (FP) is a programming paradigm that treats computation as the evaluation of mathematical functions and avoids changing state or mutable data. It focuses on writing pure, declarative functions that describe what to do, rather than the imperative approach of specifying how to do it.

At its core, functional programming emphasizes the following principles:

Pure Functions: Functions always produce the same output for the same input and have no side effects, making them predictable and easier to test.

Example:

```javascript
Copy code
const add = (a, b) => a + b;
console.log(add(2, 3)); // Always 5
```

Immutability: Data is not changed directly. Instead, new data structures are created when modifications are needed.

Example:

```javascript
Copy code
const numbers = [1, 2, 3];
const newNumbers = [...numbers, 4]; // Original array remains unchanged
```

First-Class and Higher-Order Functions:

Functions are treated as first-class citizens, meaning they can be passed as arguments, returned from other functions, or assigned to variables. Higher-order functions operate on other functions.

Example:

javascript
Copy code

```javascript
const greet = (name) => `Hello, ${name}`;
const processGreeting = (func, name) => func(name);
console.log(processGreeting(greet, 'Alice')); // "Hello, Alice"
```

Function Composition: Combining simple functions to build more complex ones.

Functional programming is widely used in JavaScript for handling tasks like data transformations (map, filter, reduce), asynchronous operations, and state management. Its declarative style leads to cleaner, modular, and more maintainable code.

1.2 Benefits of Functional Programming in JavaScript

Functional Programming (FP) brings several advantages to JavaScript development, particularly for creating clean, maintainable, and scalable applications. Here are some key benefits:

1. Improved Code Readability and Maintainability

FP emphasizes pure functions and immutability, making code easier to understand and reason about.
Declarative programming focuses on what to do rather than how, reducing complexity.
Modular functions allow for better organization and reusability.

Example:

```javascript
Copy code
const double = (x) => x * 2;
const numbers = [1, 2, 3];
```

```
const doubledNumbers = numbers.map(double);
console.log(doubledNumbers); // [2, 4, 6]
```

2. Predictable Behavior

Pure functions always return the same output for the same input, leading to predictable and testable code.
Avoiding side effects minimizes bugs caused by shared state or unexpected mutations.

3. Enhanced Debugging and Testing

Functions are isolated, making them easier to test independently.
Debugging is simplified because functions don't depend on or alter external states.

Example:

```javascript
Copy code
const add = (a, b) => a + b; // Simple, testable, and predictable
```

4. Reusability and Modularity

Small, single-purpose functions can be composed to build complex logic.
Functions can be reused across different parts of the application or even across projects.

5. Concurrency and Parallelism

Immutability ensures that data is not altered by multiple processes, making FP inherently safe for concurrent programming.

6. Simplified Asynchronous Programming

JavaScript's higher-order functions (map, reduce, filter) and libraries like RxJS leverage FP for managing asynchronous data streams.
FP techniques fit well with JavaScript's Promise and async/await constructs.

7. Better Integration with Modern JavaScript Frameworks

Frameworks like React heavily use FP principles, such as immutability and pure functions, for state management and component rendering.

Example:

javascript

Copy code

```
const Component = ({ name }) => <h1>Hello, {name}!</h1>;
```

By applying functional programming in JavaScript, developers can build robust, maintainable, and efficient applications while minimizing common pitfalls of traditional imperative programming.

1.3 Functional vs. Imperative Programming

Functional programming (FP) and imperative programming are two distinct paradigms with different approaches to solving problems and writing code. Understanding their differences helps developers choose the right paradigm for specific tasks.

1. Definition

Functional Programming: Focuses on what to do by using pure functions and avoiding side effects. It emphasizes immutability, declarative logic, and higher-order functions.

Imperative Programming: Focuses on how to do tasks by defining explicit steps and altering program state. It involves mutable variables, loops, and commands.

2. Key Characteristics

Aspect	Functional Programming	Imperative Programming
State Management	Immutable state	Mutable state
Code Style	Declarative: Describes the desired outcome	Procedural: Describes the steps needed
Functions	Pure, reusable, and stateless	

		May have side effects and alter state
Focus	What to do (logic)	How to do it (process)
Control Flow	Higher-order functions (e.g., map, reduce)	Loops (for, while)

3. Examples

Functional Approach:

```javascript
Copy code
const numbers = [1, 2, 3, 4, 5];
const doubled = numbers.map((num) => num * 2);
console.log(doubled); // [2, 4, 6, 8, 10]
```

Imperative Approach:

```javascript
Copy code
const numbers = [1, 2, 3, 4, 5];
const doubled = [];
for (let i = 0; i < numbers.length; i++) {
  doubled.push(numbers[i] * 2);
}
console.log(doubled); // [2, 4, 6, 8, 10]
```

4. Advantages of Each

Functional Programming:

Easier debugging and testing due to pure functions.
More concise and readable code for data transformations.
Safer for concurrency and parallelism.

Imperative Programming:

Better suited for tasks requiring step-by-step instructions.
Easier to grasp for beginners due to its straightforward nature.
More flexible for performance-critical applications.

5. Use Cases

Functional Programming:

Data transformations, mathematical computations, UI rendering (e.g., React).

Imperative Programming:

Tasks requiring precise control, such as algorithm implementations and low-level system programming.

Both paradigms have strengths and weaknesses. Modern JavaScript often blends functional and imperative approaches, allowing developers to leverage the best of both worlds.

Chapter 2
Core Concepts of Functional Programming

Functional Programming (FP) revolves around a set of core principles that ensure code is predictable, maintainable, and efficient. Here are the foundational concepts:

1. Pure Functions

A pure function always produces the same output for the same input and does not have side effects.

Example:
javascript
Copy code
```javascript
const square = (x) => x * x;
console.log(square(4)); // Always 16
```

2. Immutability

Data is never modified directly; instead, new data structures are created when changes are needed.

Example:
javascript
Copy code
```
const numbers = [1, 2, 3];
const updated = [...numbers, 4];
console.log(numbers); // [1, 2, 3] (unchanged)
```

3. First-Class Functions

Functions are treated as first-class citizens, meaning they can be assigned to variables, passed as arguments, and returned from other functions.

Example:

javascript
Copy code
```
const greet = () => "Hello!";
const display = (func) => console.log(func());
display(greet); // "Hello!"
```

4. Higher-Order Functions

Functions that accept other functions as arguments or return functions. These are essential for operations like mapping, filtering, and reducing data.

Example:
javascript
Copy code
```
const numbers = [1, 2, 3];
const doubled = numbers.map((x) => x * 2);
console.log(doubled); // [2, 4, 6]
```

5. Function Composition

Combining smaller functions to build more complex functionality. This improves code modularity and reuse.

Example:

javascript
Copy code
```
const add = (x) => x + 2;
const multiply = (x) => x * 3;
const compose = (f, g) => (x) => f(g(x));
const addThenMultiply = compose(multiply, add);
```

console.log(addThenMultiply(2)); // (2 + 2) * 3 − 12

6. Avoiding Side Effects

A function avoids modifying external variables or states, ensuring predictable outcomes.

Example:
javascript
Copy code
let count = 0; // Avoid modifying global variables
const increment = (x) => x + 1;
count = increment(count); // Safer and predictable

These principles are the backbone of FP, enabling developers to write modular, reusable, and bug-free code in JavaScript.

2.1 Pure Functions

A pure function is a key concept in functional programming. It is a function that adheres to the following principles:

Deterministic Behavior: A pure function always produces the same output for the same input.

No Side Effects: A pure function does not modify any external state or interact with the outside world, such as modifying variables, making API calls, or logging to the console.
These properties make pure functions predictable, easy to test, and reliable.

Characteristics of Pure Functions

Same Input, Same Output:

The result of a pure function depends solely on its arguments.

```javascript
Copy code
const add = (a, b) => a + b;
console.log(add(2, 3)); // Always 5
```

console.log(add(2, 3)); // Still 5

No External Dependencies:

Pure functions do not rely on or alter external state.

javascript
Copy code
```
let multiplier = 2; // Impure, as it depends on an external variable
const multiplyPure = (x) => x * 2; // Pure, as it has no external dependencies
```

No Side Effects:

They don't perform actions like updating a database, modifying global variables, or interacting with I/O.

javascript
Copy code
```
// Impure: modifies an external variable
let count = 0;
const incrementImpure = () => count++;

// Pure: does not alter external variables
```

```javascript
const incrementPure = (num) => num + 1;
console.log(incrementPure(5)); // Always 6
```

Advantages of Pure Functions

Predictability: The outcome of a pure function is always the same for given inputs.

Testability: Pure functions are easier to test because they don't depend on external states.

Reusability: Since they don't rely on a specific context, pure functions can be reused in different parts of the program.

Concurrency Safety: Pure functions don't interact with shared states, making them safer in multi-threaded environments.

Example in JavaScript

Impure Function:

```javascript
Copy code
```

```javascript
let discount = 0.1;
const calculatePrice = (price) => price - price * discount; // Depends on external state
```

Pure Function:

```javascript
Copy code
const calculatePrice = (price, discount) => price - price * discount; // Pure and predictable
console.log(calculatePrice(100, 0.1)); // 90
```

By using pure functions, developers can write reliable, maintainable, and modular code that is less prone to errors.

2.2 Immutability

Immutability is a core principle of functional programming that refers to the idea that once a data structure is created, it cannot be changed. Instead of modifying the original object, new objects are created to represent the updated state.

This approach ensures predictability, reduces bugs, and makes code easier to understand and maintain.

Why Immutability Matters

Predictability: Immutable data cannot be unexpectedly modified, making program behavior more predictable.

Concurrency Safety: Immutable objects are inherently thread-safe since they can't be modified, eliminating race conditions.

Debugging Simplicity: With no unexpected state changes, tracking bugs becomes easier.

Undo/Redo Features: Immutable data makes it simple to implement features like undo/redo or time-travel debugging (e.g., in React-Redux).

Working with Immutability in JavaScript

Immutable Primitives:

Primitive types like string, number, and boolean are already immutable in JavaScript.

javascript
Copy code

```
let name = "Alice";
let newName = name.toUpperCase(); // Returns a new string
console.log(name); // "Alice" remains unchanged
console.log(newName); // "ALICE"
```

Mutable Data Structures:

Data structures like objects and arrays are mutable by default, but you can work with them immutably.

Using Spread Syntax:

javascript
Copy code

```
const numbers = [1, 2, 3];
const updatedNumbers = [...numbers, 4]; // Adds 4 without modifying the original array
console.log(numbers); // [1, 2, 3] (unchanged)
console.log(updatedNumbers); // [1, 2, 3, 4]
```

Using Object Spread:

```javascript
Copy code
const user = { name: "Alice", age: 25 };
const updatedUser = { ...user, age: 26 }; // Creates a
new object
console.log(user); // { name: "Alice", age: 25 }
(unchanged)
console.log(updatedUser); // { name: "Alice", age: 26 }
```

Using Libraries for Deep Immutability:

Libraries like Immutable.js, Immer, or Lodash offer tools to handle deeply nested structures immutably.

Example with Immer:

```javascript
Copy code
import produce from "immer";

const state = { user: { name: "Alice", age: 25 } };
const newState = produce(state, (draft) => {
```

```
  draft.user.age = 26;
});
```

```
console.log(state); // Original state remains unchanged
console.log(newState); // Updated state
```

Benefits of Immutability

Prevents Side Effects: No accidental modifications to shared data.

Facilitates Functional Programming: Encourages pure functions and predictable behavior.

Enhances Debugging: Immutable data helps maintain a clear history of changes.

By practicing immutability, developers can build robust, error-free applications while maintaining clarity and consistency in their codebase.

2.3 First-Class Functions

In JavaScript, first-class functions mean that functions are treated as first-class citizens. This concept allows functions to be used like any other value:

They can be assigned to variables.
Passed as arguments to other functions.
Returned as values from other functions.
This characteristic is a cornerstone of functional programming and enables powerful abstractions like higher-order functions and callbacks.

Key Characteristics of First-Class Functions

Functions as Variables:

Functions can be stored in variables or constants.

```javascript
Copy code
const greet = () => "Hello, World!";
console.log(greet()); // "Hello, World!"
```

Functions as Arguments:

Functions can be passed to other functions as parameters.

javascript
Copy code

```javascript
const sayHello = (name) => `Hello, ${name}!`;
const processGreeting = (func, name) => func(name);
console.log(processGreeting(sayHello,    "Alice"));    // "Hello, Alice!"
```

Functions as Return Values:

Functions can return other functions.

javascript
Copy code

```javascript
const multiplyBy = (factor) => (number) => number * factor;
const double = multiplyBy(2);
console.log(double(5)); // 10
```

Functions as Properties of Objects:

Functions can be stored in objects as properties or methods.

javascript
Copy code

```
const calculator = {
  add: (a, b) => a + b,
  subtract: (a, b) => a - b,
};
console.log(calculator.add(5, 3)); // 8
```

Applications of First-Class Functions

Higher-Order Functions:

Functions that take other functions as arguments or return them.

javascript
Copy code
```
const numbers = [1, 2, 3, 4];
const squared = numbers.map((num) => num * num);
console.log(squared); // [1, 4, 9, 16]
```

Callbacks:

Functions passed as arguments to be executed later.

javascript
Copy code

setTimeout(() => console.log("Hello after 2 seconds"), 2000);

Closures:

Functions that capture variables from their surrounding scope.

javascript
Copy code
```javascript
const makeCounter = () => {
  let count = 0;
  return () => ++count;
};
const counter = makeCounter();
console.log(counter()); // 1
console.log(counter()); // 2
```

Advantages of First-Class Functions

Flexibility: Functions can be passed and returned dynamically, enabling modular and reusable code.

Higher Abstractions: They allow for concepts like event handling, currying, and functional composition.

Readability and Conciseness: Simplifies operations like mapping, filtering, and reducing data.

Example of First-Class Functions in Functional Programming

```javascript
Copy code
const applyOperation = (operation, a, b) => operation(a, b);
const add = (x, y) => x + y;
const multiply = (x, y) => x * y;

console.log(applyOperation(add, 2, 3)); // 5
console.log(applyOperation(multiply, 2, 3)); // 6
```

First-class functions make JavaScript a flexible and expressive language, particularly for functional programming.

2.4 Higher-Order Functions

A higher-order function (HOF) is a function that either:

Takes one or more functions as arguments.
Returns a function as a result.
In functional programming, higher-order functions are a powerful concept because they enable abstraction and enable operations like function composition, currying, and transformations of data structures. Since functions in JavaScript are first-class citizens, they can be passed around as values, making HOFs a natural part of the language.

Key Characteristics of Higher-Order Functions

Accepting Functions as Arguments:
HOFs can take one or more functions as parameters to perform operations on them.

Example:

javascript
Copy code
```
const greet = (name) => `Hello, ${name}!`;
const processGreeting = (func, name) => func(name);
```

```javascript
console.log(processGreeting(greet, "Alice")); // "Hello, Alice!"
```

Returning Functions:

A higher-order function can return a new function. Example:

```javascript
Copy code
const multiplyBy = (factor) => (number) => number * factor;
const double = multiplyBy(2);
console.log(double(5)); // 10
```

Using Functions to Modify Behavior:

HOFs can be used to modify or extend the behavior of other functions.

Example:

```javascript
Copy code
const withLogging = (fn) => {
```

```javascript
  return (...args) => {
    console.log(`Calling with args: ${args}`);
    const result = fn(...args);
    console.log(`Result: ${result}`);
    return result;
  };
};

const add = (a, b) => a + b;
const addWithLogging = withLogging(add);
console.log(addWithLogging(2, 3)); // Logs arguments
and result
```

Common Examples of Higher-Order Functions in JavaScript

Array Methods:

JavaScript provides several built-in higher-order functions, like map(), filter(), reduce(), and forEach(), which are used to transform or process data in arrays.

map: Transforms each element in the array.

javascript

Copy code
```javascript
const numbers = [1, 2, 3];
const doubled = numbers.map(num => num * 2);
console.log(doubled); // [2, 4, 6]
```

filter: Filters elements based on a condition.

javascript
Copy code
```javascript
const numbers = [1, 2, 3, 4, 5];
const evenNumbers = numbers.filter(num => num % 2 === 0);
console.log(evenNumbers); // [2, 4]
```

reduce: Reduces the array to a single value by applying a function.

javascript
Copy code
```javascript
const numbers = [1, 2, 3, 4];
const sum = numbers.reduce((total, num) => total + num, 0);
console.log(sum); // 10
```

Function Composition:

Combining two or more functions to create a new function.

Example:

javascript
Copy code

```javascript
const add = (x) => x + 2;
const multiply = (x) => x * 3;

const compose = (f, g) => (x) => f(g(x));
const addThenMultiply = compose(multiply, add);
console.log(addThenMultiply(2)); // (2 + 2) * 3 = 12
```

Currying:

Currying is the process of transforming a function that takes multiple arguments into a series of functions that each take a single argument.

Example:

javascript
Copy code

```javascript
const multiply = (x) => (y) => x * y;
```

```
const multiplyBy2 = multiply(2);
console.log(multiplyBy2(5)); // 10
```

Benefits of Higher-Order Functions

Abstraction:

HOFs allow for more abstract and reusable code. They can simplify logic by separating concerns and improving readability.

Flexibility:

Functions can be customized or extended dynamically, making the codebase flexible and easy to modify.

Composability:

Functions can be combined to build complex behavior, leading to cleaner and more modular code.

Improved Code Reusability:

HOFs allow for creating generalized functions that can work with different operations, making them reusable across various scenarios.

Example of a Higher-Order Function

A typical use case for a higher-order function might involve logging or caching behavior. Here is a function that adds caching to an existing function:

```javascript
Copy code
const cache = (fn) => {
  const results = {};
  return (arg) => {
    if (results[arg]) {
      return results[arg]; // Return cached result
    }
    const result = fn(arg);
    results[arg] = result; // Cache the result
    return result;
  };
};

const square = (n) => n * n;
```

```
const cachedSquare = cache(square);
console.log(cachedSquare(4)); // 16 (calculated)
console.log(cachedSquare(4)); // 16 (cached)
```

In this example, cache() is a higher-order function that wraps the square() function, allowing it to cache results for previously seen inputs.

Higher-order functions are fundamental to functional programming in JavaScript. By enabling dynamic behavior and abstraction, they make your code more flexible, concise, and reusable.

2.5 Function Composition

Function composition is the process of combining multiple functions to create a new function. In functional programming, it allows for the construction of complex operations by combining simpler functions. The output of one function becomes the input of another, allowing for more modular, reusable, and declarative code.

In JavaScript, function composition is a powerful tool that encourages a functional approach to problem-solving.

How Function Composition Works

Given two functions, f and g, the composition of these two functions, denoted as f ∘ g, means that you apply g first, then pass its result into f.

Mathematically:

$(f \circ g)(x) = f(g(x))$

This means you first apply g(x) and then apply f to the result of g(x).

In JavaScript, the composition of two functions can be implemented as:

```javascript
Copy code
const compose = (f, g) => (x) => f(g(x));
```

Example of Function Composition

Let's say you have two simple functions, add and multiply, and you want to compose them to create a new function that first multiplies a number and then adds a constant to the result.

```javascript
Copy code
const add = (x) => x + 2;
const multiply = (x) => x * 3;

const compose = (f, g) => (x) => f(g(x));

const addThenMultiply = compose(multiply, add);

console.log(addThenMultiply(2)); // (2 + 2) * 3 = 12
```

In this example:

add(2) returns 4.
multiply(4) returns 12.
The composed function, addThenMultiply(2), first adds 2 to 2, and then multiplies the result by 3.

Function Composition with Multiple Functions

You can compose multiple functions together to create more complex pipelines of transformations. Here's an example with more than two functions:

javascript
Copy code

```
const subtract = (x) => x - 1;
const divide = (x) => x / 2;

const compose = (f, g) => (x) => f(g(x));

const complexOperation = compose(subtract, compose(divide, multiply));

console.log(complexOperation(6)); // First multiply(6), then divide, then subtract
```

In this case, the order of composition matters, and you apply multiply, then divide, and finally subtract to the initial input.

Composing Functions with Curried Functions

When dealing with curried functions, function composition is even more powerful. Curried functions return other functions, and they can be composed with ease. Here's an example of curried function composition:

javascript
Copy code
```javascript
const multiplyBy = (x) => (y) => y * x;
const addTo = (x) => (y) => y + x;

const compose = (f, g) => (x) => f(g(x));

const multiplyBy2 = multiplyBy(2);
const add5 = addTo(5);

const add5ThenMultiplyBy2 = compose(multiplyBy2, add5);

console.log(add5ThenMultiplyBy2(3)); // (3 + 5) * 2 = 16
```

Here, we compose two curried functions (multiplyBy and addTo), resulting in a new function that first adds 5 to the number and then multiplies the result by 2.

Benefits of Function Composition

Modularity:

Composition allows breaking down complex problems into smaller, simpler functions, which are easier to test, maintain, and debug.

Reusability:

Small, pure functions can be reused in different contexts, making your codebase more flexible and efficient.

Declarative Code:

Composing functions results in more declarative code that focuses on "what to do" rather than "how to do it". This leads to cleaner and easier-to-read code.

Code Readability:
Function composition enables chaining operations, making the flow of data through transformations clear and easy to follow.

Avoiding Side Effects:

Function composition encourages the use of pure functions, which don't alter external state, making your code more predictable and less error-prone.

Real-World Example: Data Transformation Pipeline

Function composition is widely used in scenarios like data transformation pipelines or processing streams of data. For instance, consider a pipeline that processes an array of numbers:

```javascript
Copy code
const numbers = [1, 2, 3, 4, 5];

const add = (x) => x + 1;
const square = (x) => x * x;
const divide = (x) => x / 2;

const compose = (f, g) => (x) => f(g(x));

const pipeline = compose(divide, compose(square, add));
```

```
const result = numbers.map(pipeline);
console.log(result); // [1, 4, 9, 16, 25] -> add 1, square,
then divide by 2
```

In this example, we are transforming an array of numbers through a series of functions: adding 1, squaring the result, and then dividing by 2. This is a common pattern in data transformation, especially in frameworks like React (with JSX transformations or Redux middlewares).

Conclusion

Function composition enables the creation of complex behaviors from simple functions, resulting in clean, modular, and reusable code. By applying composition, developers can construct flexible pipelines and abstractions, improving both readability and maintainability in their programs. It's a fundamental technique in functional programming and a key tool for any JavaScript developer looking to write elegant and efficient code.

Chapter 3
Modern JavaScript Techniques

Modern JavaScript has evolved significantly with the introduction of ES6 (ECMAScript 2015) and subsequent updates, bringing powerful features and techniques that improve performance, readability, and maintainability. Here's a brief overview of some key modern JavaScript techniques:

1. Arrow Functions

Simpler and more concise syntax for writing functions.

```javascript
Copy code
// Traditional Function
function add(a, b) {
  return a + b;
}
```

```javascript
// Arrow Function
const add = (a, b) => a + b;
```

2. Destructuring Assignment

Extract values from arrays or properties from objects into variables.

```javascript
javascript
Copy code
const user = { name: "Alice", age: 25 };

// Object Destructuring
const { name, age } = user;

// Array Destructuring
const numbers = [1, 2, 3];
const [first, second] = numbers;
```

3. Spread and Rest Operators

The spread operator (...) is used to expand arrays or objects, while the rest operator collects multiple elements into an array.

```javascript
Copy code
// Spread
const arr1 = [1, 2];
const arr2 = [...arr1, 3, 4]; // [1, 2, 3, 4]

// Rest
const sum = (...nums) => nums.reduce((total, num) => total + num, 0);
console.log(sum(1, 2, 3)); // 6
```

4. Template Literals

Enable multi-line strings and embedding expressions.

```javascript
Copy code
const name = "Alice";
const message = `Hello, ${name}! Welcome to JavaScript.`;
```

53

5. Modules (ES Modules)

Support for importing and exporting code between files.

```javascript
Copy code
// Exporting (module.js)
export const greet = (name) => `Hello, ${name}!`;

// Importing
import { greet } from './module.js';
console.log(greet("Alice")); // Hello, Alice!
```

6. Promises and Async/Await

Handle asynchronous operations more cleanly.

```javascript
Copy code
// Promises
fetch("https://api.example.com")
  .then((response) => response.json())
  .then((data) => console.log(data));
```

```javascript
// Async/Await
const fetchData = async () => {
        const        response        =        await
fetch("https://api.example.com");
  const data = await response.json();
  console.log(data);
};
```

7. Default Parameters

Specify default values for function parameters.

javascript
Copy code
```javascript
const greet = (name = "Guest") => `Hello, ${name}!`;
console.log(greet()); // Hello, Guest!
```

8. Optional Chaining and Nullish Coalescing
Simplify working with deeply nested objects and handle null
or undefined values.

javascript
Copy code

```javascript
const user = { profile: { name: "Alice" } };
console.log(user?.profile?.name); // Alice

const value = null ?? "Default Value";
console.log(value); // Default Value
```

9. Object and Array Methods

Modern methods like map(), filter(), reduce(), find(), some(), and every() enhance functional programming.

javascript
Copy code
```javascript
const numbers = [1, 2, 3, 4];
const evenNumbers = numbers.filter((num) => num % 2 === 0);
console.log(evenNumbers); // [2, 4]
```

10. Classes and Enhanced Object Literals

Provide a cleaner syntax for working with objects and inheritance.

javascript
Copy code

```
class Person {
  constructor(name) {
    this.name = name;
  }
  greet() {
    return `Hello, ${this.name}!`;
  }
}
```

```
const alice = new Person("Alice");
console.log(alice.greet()); // Hello, Alice!
```

By leveraging these modern JavaScript techniques, developers can write cleaner, more efficient, and maintainable code while enhancing application performance and user experience.

3.1 Arrow Functions

Arrow functions, introduced in ES6 (ECMAScript 2015), are a concise way to write functions in JavaScript. They provide a shorter syntax compared to traditional function expressions while maintaining readability and simplifying certain use cases.

Syntax

The syntax of an arrow function uses the => symbol (often called a "fat arrow"):

javascript
Copy code
```
const add = (a, b) => a + b;
```

This is equivalent to:

javascript
Copy code
```
function add(a, b) {
  return a + b;
}
```

Key Features of Arrow Functions

Shorter Syntax:

Arrow functions reduce boilerplate code, especially for simple one-liners.

javascript

Copy code

```javascript
// Traditional function
const square = function (x) {
  return x * x;
};

// Arrow function
const square = (x) => x * x;
```

Implicit Return:

If the function body consists of a single expression, the result of the expression is returned automatically without needing a return keyword.

javascript

Copy code

```javascript
const double = (x) => x * 2; // Implicit return
```

No this Binding:

Arrow functions do not have their own this. Instead, they inherit this from the surrounding lexical scope. This makes them especially useful in callbacks and event handlers.

```javascript
Copy code
function Person(name) {
  this.name = name;
}

Person.prototype.greet = function () {
  setTimeout(() => {
    console.log(`Hello, ${this.name}`);
  }, 1000);
};

const alice = new Person("Alice");
alice.greet(); // "Hello, Alice" after 1 second
```

If a traditional function were used instead of an arrow function, the value of this would be undefined or refer to the global object, causing unexpected behavior.

No arguments Object:

Arrow functions do not have their own arguments object. To access arguments in an arrow function, you must use rest parameters.

javascript
Copy code
const sum = (...args) => args.reduce((total, num) => total + num, 0);
console.log(sum(1, 2, 3)); // 6

When to Use Arrow Functions

Callbacks:

Arrow functions are ideal for callbacks in array methods like map, filter, and reduce.

javascript
Copy code
const numbers = [1, 2, 3];
const doubled = numbers.map((num) => num * 2);
console.log(doubled); // [2, 4, 6]

Event Handlers:

They simplify writing event listeners without worrying about binding this.

javascript
Copy code

```
document.getElementById("button").addEventListener("click", () => {
  console.log("Button clicked!");
});
```

Functional Programming:

Arrow functions are often used in functional programming techniques like composition and currying.

javascript
Copy code

```
const add = (a) => (b) => a + b;
console.log(add(2)(3)); // 5
```

Limitations of Arrow Functions

No this, super, or new.target:

Arrow functions do not bind this, so they cannot be used as constructors or in methods that rely on their own this.

javascript
Copy code
```
const MyClass = () => {};
const obj = new MyClass(); // Error: MyClass is not a constructor
```

Not Suitable for Methods in Object Literals:

Arrow functions should not be used for defining methods in object literals because they do not bind their own this.

javascript
Copy code
```
const obj = {
  name: "Alice",
  greet: () => `Hello, ${this.name}`, // `this` is undefined
};
console.log(obj.greet()); // "Hello, undefined"
```

No arguments Object:

Arrow functions lack their own arguments object, making it necessary to use rest parameters if argument access is needed.

Examples of Arrow Functions

Simple Arrow Function:

javascript
Copy code
```javascript
const greet = (name) => `Hello, ${name}!`;
console.log(greet("Alice")); // "Hello, Alice!"
```
..
Arrow Function with No Parameters:

javascript
Copy code
```javascript
const sayHello = () => "Hello, World!";
console.log(sayHello()); // "Hello, World!"
```

Arrow Function with Multiple Lines:

Use curly braces {} for functions with more than one statement.

javascript

Copy code
```
const sum = (a, b) => {
  const result = a + b;
  return result;
};
console.log(sum(2, 3)); // 5
```

Conclusion

Arrow functions bring a modern, concise syntax to JavaScript, making code cleaner and easier to read. They are particularly useful for callbacks, functional programming, and scenarios where the lexical scoping of this simplifies code. However, they are not a replacement for traditional functions in all cases, so understanding their limitations is essential.

3.2 Spread and Rest Operators

The spread (...) and rest (...) operators, introduced in ES6 (ECMAScript 2015), provide powerful and flexible ways to work with arrays, objects, and function arguments. While they share the same syntax (...), their purposes differ based on how and where they are used.

1. Spread Operator (...)

The spread operator expands elements of an array, object, or iterable into individual elements. It is used for creating copies, merging, and passing data seamlessly.

Use Cases of the Spread Operator

Copying Arrays

Create a shallow copy of an array.

```javascript
Copy code
const numbers = [1, 2, 3];
const copy = [...numbers];
console.log(copy); // [1, 2, 3]
```

Merging Arrays

Combine multiple arrays into one.

javascript
Copy code
```javascript
const arr1 = [1, 2];
const arr2 = [3, 4];
const merged = [...arr1, ...arr2];
console.log(merged); // [1, 2, 3, 4]
```

Copying Objects

Create a shallow copy of an object.

javascript
Copy code
```javascript
const obj = { a: 1, b: 2 };
const copy = { ...obj };
console.log(copy); // { a: 1, b: 2 }
```

Merging Objects

Merge properties of multiple objects into one.

javascript
Copy code
```javascript
const obj1 = { a: 1 };
```

```javascript
const obj2 = { b: 2, c: 3 };
const merged = { ...obj1, ...obj2 };
console.log(merged); // { a: 1, b: 2, c: 3 }
```

Passing Arguments to Functions

Spread elements of an array as individual arguments to a function.

javascript
Copy code
```javascript
const numbers = [1, 2, 3];
const sum = (a, b, c) => a + b + c;
console.log(sum(...numbers)); // 6
```

2. Rest Operator (...)

The rest operator collects multiple elements or properties into a single array or object. It is often used in function arguments and destructuring.

Use Cases of the Rest Operator

Handling Variable Numbers of Function Arguments

Combine all arguments into an array.

javascript
Copy code
```javascript
const sum = (...nums) => nums.reduce((total, num) =>
total + num, 0);
console.log(sum(1, 2, 3, 4)); // 10
```

Destructuring Arrays

Collect the rest of the array into a separate variable.

javascript
Copy code
```javascript
const [first, ...rest] = [1, 2, 3, 4];
console.log(first); // 1
console.log(rest); // [2, 3, 4]
```

Destructuring Objects

Extract specific properties and collect the rest into a separate object.

javascript
Copy code

```javascript
const obj = { a: 1, b: 2, c: 3 };
const { a, ...rest } = obj;
console.log(a); // 1
console.log(rest); // { b: 2, c: 3 }
```

Default Parameters with Rest

Gather remaining arguments for flexible function definitions.

javascript
Copy code
```javascript
const greet = (greeting, ...names) => {
  return `${greeting}, ${names.join(" and ")}!`;
};
console.log(greet("Hello", "Alice", "Bob", "Charlie"));
// Hello, Alice and Bob and Charlie!
```

Key Differences Between Spread and Rest

Feature	Spread Operator (...)	Rest Operator (...)

Purpose	Expands elements into individual items.	Gathers multiple elements into a single array or object.
Context	Arrays, objects, function calls	. Function arguments, destructuring.
Position	Used in expressions to expand data.	Used in parameter lists or destructuring.

Examples of Combining Spread and Rest

Cloning and Modifying Objects

Use the spread operator to create a copy and the rest operator to exclude specific properties.

javascript

Copy code

```
const user = { name: "Alice", age: 25, country: "USA" };
const { age, ...rest } = user;
const updatedUser = { ...rest, age: 26 };
console.log(updatedUser); // { name: "Alice", country: "USA", age: 26 }
```

Flexible Function Signatures

Use rest for collecting arguments and spread for passing them.

javascript

Copy code

```
const add = (...nums) => nums.reduce((sum, num) => sum + num, 0);
const numbers = [1, 2, 3];
console.log(add(...numbers)); // 6
```

Conclusion

The spread and rest operators simplify working with arrays, objects, and arguments in JavaScript. The spread operator helps expand data into its individual elements, while the rest operator collects elements into a single structure. These operators not only enhance code readability but also improve flexibility, making them indispensable tools in modern JavaScript development.

3.3 Destructuring

Destructuring is a convenient way to extract values from arrays or properties from objects and assign them to variables. Introduced in ES6 (ECMAScript 2015), destructuring simplifies code by reducing the need for repetitive access to array indices or object properties.

1. Array Destructuring

Array destructuring allows you to unpack values from an array into variables.

Syntax
javascript
Copy code
const [var1, var2, ...rest] = array;

Examples

Basic Destructuring

javascript
Copy code
const numbers = [1, 2, 3];
const [first, second, third] = numbers;
console.log(first); // 1
console.log(second); // 2
console.log(third); // 3

Skipping Elements

Use commas to skip unwanted elements.

javascript

```
Copy code
const numbers = [1, 2, 3, 4];
const [first, , third] = numbers;
console.log(first);  // 1
console.log(third);  // 3
```

Default Values

Provide default values for variables in case the array does not have enough elements.

```javascript
Copy code
const numbers = [1];
const [first, second = 0] = numbers;
console.log(first);  // 1
console.log(second); // 0
```

Rest Operator in Destructuring
Collect the remaining elements into a new array.

```javascript
Copy code
const numbers = [1, 2, 3, 4];
```

```javascript
const [first, ...rest] = numbers;
console.log(first); // 1
console.log(rest);  // [2, 3, 4]
```

2. Object Destructuring

Object destructuring allows you to extract properties from an object and assign them to variables.

Syntax
javascript
Copy code
```javascript
const { key1, key2, ...rest } = object;
```
Examples

Basic Destructuring

javascript
Copy code
```javascript
const user = { name: "Alice", age: 25 };
const { name, age } = user;
console.log(name); // Alice
console.log(age);  // 25
```

Renaming Variables

Assign properties to variables with different names.

javascript
Copy code
```javascript
const user = { name: "Alice", age: 25 };
const { name: userName, age: userAge } = user;
console.log(userName); // Alice
console.log(userAge);  // 25
```

Default Values

Provide default values for properties that may not exist.

javascript
Copy code
```javascript
const user = { name: "Alice" };
const { name, age = 30 } = user;
console.log(name); // Alice
console.log(age);  // 30
```

Rest Operator in Objects

Collect the remaining properties into a new object.

```javascript
Copy code
const user = { name: "Alice", age: 25, country: "USA" };
const { name, ...rest } = user;
console.log(name); // Alice
console.log(rest); // { age: 25, country: "USA" }
```

3. Nested Destructuring

Destructure nested arrays or objects to access deeply nested values.

Examples

Nested Arrays

```javascript
Copy code
const numbers = [1, [2, 3], 4];
const [first, [second, third]] = numbers;
console.log(first);  // 1
console.log(second); // 2
console.log(third);  // 3
```

Nested Objects

```javascript
Copy code
const user = {
  name: "Alice",
  address: {
    city: "Wonderland",
    zip: "12345",
  },
};
const { name, address: { city, zip } } = user;
console.log(name); // Alice
console.log(city); // Wonderland
console.log(zip);  // 12345
```

4. Function Parameters Destructuring

You can destructure arrays and objects directly in function parameters for cleaner and more readable code.

Examples
Array Destructuring in Function Parameters

javascript

```
Copy code
const sum = ([a, b]) => a + b;
console.log(sum([1, 2])); // 3
```

Object Destructuring in Function Parameters

javascript
Copy code
```
const greet = ({ name, age }) => `Hello, ${name}. You
are ${age} years old.`;
console.log(greet({ name: "Alice", age: 25 }));
// Hello, Alice. You are 25 years old.
```

5. Combining Destructuring with Spread and Rest Operators

Combine destructuring with spread/rest for flexible data manipulation.

Example

javascript
Copy code
```
const user = { name: "Alice", age: 25, country: "USA" };
const { name, ...rest } = user;
```

```
const updatedUser = { ...rest, age: 26 };
console.log(updatedUser); // { age: 26, country: "USA"
}
```

Advantages of Destructuring

Cleaner Code: Reduces repetitive access to properties or indices.

Improved Readability: Makes variable assignments more explicit and readable.

Default Handling: Allows default values for undefined properties.

Powerful Patterns: Enables handling of complex nested data structures.

Conclusion

Destructuring is a versatile feature that simplifies working with arrays, objects, and function arguments. It is especially useful in modern JavaScript applications for making code concise, readable, and maintainable.

3.4 Promises and Async/Await

Handling asynchronous operations efficiently is essential in modern JavaScript development. Promises and Async/Await are two key features that simplify asynchronous programming, making code easier to read and maintain.

1. Promises

A Promise is an object that represents the eventual completion (or failure) of an asynchronous operation and its resulting value.

States of a Promise

A Promise can be in one of three states:

Pending: The initial state; the operation has not completed yet.
Fulfilled: The operation completed successfully.
Rejected: The operation failed.

Creating a Promise

A Promise is created using the Promise constructor.

```javascript
Copy code
const myPromise = new Promise((resolve, reject) => {
  const success = true;
  if (success) {
    resolve("Operation was successful");
  } else {
    reject("Operation failed");
  }
});
```

Using .then(), .catch(), and .finally()
.then(): Handles the resolved value of the promise.

.catch(): Handles errors or rejection.
.finally(): Executes after the promise is settled, regardless of success or failure.

```javascript
Copy code
myPromise
```

```javascript
  .then((result) => console.log(result)) // "Operation
was successful"
  .catch((error) => console.error(error))
  .finally(() => console.log("Operation complete"));
```

Chaining Promises

Promises can be chained to perform sequential asynchronous operations.

javascript
Copy code
```javascript
fetch("https://api.example.com/data")
  .then((response) => response.json())
  .then((data) => console.log(data))
  .catch((error) => console.error(error));
```

2. Async/Await

Introduced in ES8 (ES2017), Async/Await is a syntactic sugar built on top of Promises. It provides a cleaner and more readable way to work with asynchronous code.

Key Features

Async Functions: Declared using the async keyword and always return a Promise.

Await Keyword: Pauses the execution of an async function until the Promise is resolved or rejected.

Syntax

javascript

Copy code

```
async function fetchData() {
  const response = await fetch("https://api.example.com/data");
  const data = await response.json();
  console.log(data);
}
```

Error Handling with Try/Catch

Async/Await allows error handling using try and catch blocks.

javascript

Copy code

```
async function fetchData() {
  try {
```

```javascript
    const response = await
fetch("https://api.example.com/data");
    const data = await response.json();
    console.log(data);
  } catch (error) {
    console.error("Error fetching data:", error);
  }
}
fetchData();
```

Executing Multiple Promises with Promise.all

Use Promise.all to execute multiple promises concurrently.

```javascript
Copy code
async function fetchMultipleData() {
  try {
    const [data1, data2] = await Promise.all([
        fetch("https://api.example.com/data1").then((res)
=> res.json()),
        fetch("https://api.example.com/data2").then((res)
=> res.json()),
    ]);
    console.log(data1, data2);
```

```
  } catch (error) {
    console.error("Error fetching data:", error);
  }
}
fetchMultipleData();
```

Comparison of Promises and Async/Await

Feature	Promises	Async/Await
Syntax	Chain-based (.then(), .catch()).	Cleaner, sequential flow using await.
Error Handling	Handled with .catch().	Handled with try/catch.
Readability	Can become complex with nested .then()	More readable and less nested
Concurrency	Requires Promise.all for parallel tasks	Easily handled with Promise.all.

When to Use Promises vs. Async/Await

Use Promises when:

You are working with older JavaScript environments that may not support async/await.
You need to perform complex chaining of asynchronous tasks.

Use Async/Await when:

You need readable and maintainable code for sequential asynchronous tasks.

You want better error handling using try/catch.

Examples of Real-World Usage
Fetching API Data

Using Promises:

javascript
Copy code

```javascript
fetch("https://api.example.com/data")
  .then((response) => response.json())
  .then((data) => console.log(data))
  .catch((error) => console.error(error));
```

Using Async/Await:

javascript
Copy code

```javascript
async function fetchData() {
  try {
    const response = await fetch("https://api.example.com/data");
    const data = await response.json();
    console.log(data);
  } catch (error) {
    console.error("Error:", error);
  }
}
fetchData();
```

Simulating Delayed Execution

Using Promises:

```javascript
Copy code
const delay = (ms) => new Promise((resolve) =>
setTimeout(resolve, ms));
delay(1000).then(() => console.log("1 second delay"));
```

Using Async/Await:

```javascript
Copy code
const delay = (ms) => new Promise((resolve) =>
setTimeout(resolve, ms));
async function runDelay() {
  await delay(1000);
  console.log("1 second delay");
}
runDelay();
```

Conclusion

Both Promises and Async/Await are essential for asynchronous programming in JavaScript. While Promises provide a robust foundation, Async/Await enhances code readability and maintainability by offering a synchronous-like structure for asynchronous operations. Understanding when and how to use each approach allows developers to write cleaner, more efficient code.

3.5 Modules and Imports

Modules in JavaScript allow developers to split code into reusable, maintainable, and logically organized files. Introduced as part of ES6 (ES2015), modules make it easier to share code between files and manage dependencies in modern applications.

What Are Modules?

A module is a self-contained block of reusable code, typically stored in its own file. It encapsulates functionality and exposes specific parts of the code for use in other files via exports.

1. Exporting from Modules

You can export values, functions, objects, or classes from a module to make them available to other files.

Named Exports

Export multiple values with unique names.

javascript
Copy code

```javascript
// math.js
export const add = (a, b) => a + b;
export const subtract = (a, b) => a - b;
```

Default Export

Export a single default value or function from a module.

javascript
Copy code

```javascript
// utils.js
export default function greet(name) {
  return `Hello, ${name}!`;
```

}

2. Importing Modules

To use exported values in another file, you import them.

Importing Named Exports

Use curly braces to import specific exports.

```javascript
// main.js
import { add, subtract } from './math.js';

console.log(add(2, 3));     // 5
console.log(subtract(5, 2)); // 3
```

Importing Default Exports

No curly braces are needed for default exports. You can assign any name to the imported value.

```javascript
```

```javascript
// main.js
import greet from './utils.js';

console.log(greet("Alice"));  // Hello, Alice!
```

Renaming Imports

Rename imports to avoid naming conflicts.

javascript
Copy code
```javascript
import { add as addition, subtract as subtraction } from './math.js';

console.log(addition(4, 2));   // 6
console.log(subtraction(4, 2));// 2
```

Importing All Exports

Use * to import all named exports as an object.

javascript
Copy code
```javascript
import * as math from './math.js';
```

```javascript
console.log(math.add(3, 2));     // 5
console.log(math.subtract(3, 2)); // 1
```

3. Combining Named and Default Exports

A module can have both named and default exports.

javascript
Copy code
```javascript
// math.js
export const multiply = (a, b) => a * b;
export default function divide(a, b) {
  return a / b;
}
```

Importing both in another file:

javascript
Copy code
```javascript
// main.js
import divide, { multiply } from './math.js';

console.log(multiply(3, 4)); // 12
console.log(divide(8, 2));   // 4
```

4. Dynamic Imports

Dynamic imports allow importing modules at runtime using the import() function. This is useful for lazy-loading or conditionally loading modules.

Example

javascript
Copy code

```javascript
if (someCondition) {
  import('./math.js')
    .then((module) => {
      console.log(module.add(2, 3)); // 5
    })
    .catch((error) => console.error(error));
}
```

With async/await:

javascript
Copy code

```javascript
async function loadMath() {
  const math = await import('./math.js');
  console.log(math.add(2, 3)); // 5
```

```
}
loadMath();
```

5. Benefits of Using Modules

Code Reusability: Break code into smaller, reusable components.

Maintainability: Logical separation improves readability and reduces complexity.

Dependency Management: Clearly defines dependencies between different parts of the application.

Avoiding Global Scope Pollution: Keeps variables and functions local to the module.
Lazy Loading: Dynamically load modules only when needed, improving performance.

6. Using Modules in Browsers

Browsers natively support ES6 modules. To use them:

Save files with the .js extension.
Use the type="module" attribute in the <script> tag.

Example

html

Copy code

```html
<script type="module">
  import { add } from './math.js';
  console.log(add(2, 3));
</script>
```

7. Using Modules in Node.js

In Node.js, modules are managed with CommonJS or ES Modules.

CommonJS: Uses require and module.exports.
ES Modules: Uses import and export. Enabled in Node.js by adding "type": "module" to package.json.

Example: CommonJS

javascript

Copy code

```javascript
// math.js
exports.add = (a, b) => a + b;
```

```javascript
// main.js
const math = require('./math.js');
console.log(math.add(2, 3)); // 5
```

Example: ES Modules
javascript
Copy code
```javascript
// math.js
export const add = (a, b) => a + b;

// main.js
import { add } from './math.js';
console.log(add(2, 3)); // 5
```

Best Practices for Using Modules

Use Default Exports for Single Responsibility
If a file has one main functionality, use export default.

Prefer Named Exports for Multiple Utilities
Use named exports for utility functions or constants.

Organize Module Files

Group related modules into directories for better structure.

Avoid Circular Dependencies

Ensure modules do not depend on each other in a loop.

Conclusion

Modules and imports are essential features for building scalable and maintainable JavaScript applications. By encapsulating functionality, defining clear dependencies, and promoting reusability, they enable developers to write cleaner, modular, and efficient code. Whether you're working on the front end or back end, understanding and leveraging JavaScript modules is critical for modern development.

Chapter 4
Functional Programming in JavaScript

Functional programming (FP) is a programming paradigm that treats computation as the evaluation of mathematical functions and avoids changing state or mutable data. It emphasizes writing pure, predictable functions that are easy to test and maintain.

Key Principles of Functional Programming

Pure Functions: Functions that always produce the same output for the same input and have no side effects.

javascript
Copy code
```
const add = (a, b) => a + b; // Pure function
```

Immutability: Data is never modified directly. Instead, new copies are created with changes.

javascript
Copy code
```
const array = [1, 2, 3];
```

const newArray = [...array, 4]; // **Original array remains unchanged**

First-Class Functions: Functions are treated as values that can be assigned to variables, passed as arguments, or returned from other functions.

javascript
Copy code
```
const greet = () => "Hello";
const sayHello = greet; // Assigning a function to a variable
```

Higher-Order Functions: Functions that take other functions as arguments or return them.

javascript
Copy code
```
const applyTwice = (fn, value) => fn(fn(value));
```

Function Composition: Combining smaller functions to build more complex functions.

javascript
Copy code

```javascript
const compose = (f, g) => (x) => f(g(x));
```

Benefits of Functional Programming in JavaScript

Predictable Code: Pure functions and immutability reduce bugs.

Reusability: Modular, small functions are easier to reuse.

Testability: Pure functions are simple to test.

Concurrency: Immutability prevents issues in concurrent environments.

Readability: Declarative code is often easier to understand.

Examples of Functional Programming in JavaScript

Array Methods: Functional programming concepts are built into JavaScript's array methods like .map(), .filter(), and .reduce().

```javascript
Copy code
const numbers = [1, 2, 3, 4];
const doubled = numbers.map((n) => n * 2); // [2, 4, 6, 8]
```

Using reduce for Aggregation:

javascript
Copy code

```javascript
const sum = numbers.reduce((total, num) => total + num, 0); // 10
```

Currying: Breaking down a function that takes multiple arguments into a series of functions that each take one argument.

javascript
Copy code

```javascript
const multiply = (a) => (b) => a * b;
const double = multiply(2);
console.log(double(3)); // 6
```

Conclusion

Functional programming in JavaScript leverages its first-class and higher-order functions to write clean, maintainable, and bug-resistant code. By focusing on immutability and pure functions, developers can build robust and scalable applications.

4.1 Using map(), filter(), and reduce()

JavaScript's array methods map(), filter(), and reduce() are powerful tools for functional programming. These methods allow you to work with arrays in a declarative and concise way, enabling efficient transformations, filtering, and aggregation of data.

1. map()

The map() method creates a new array by applying a callback function to each element of the original array.

Syntax

javascript

Copy code

array.map(callback(element, index, array), thisArg);

callback: A function executed on each element.

thisArg: (Optional) Value to use as this when executing the callback.

Example: Doubling Numbers

javascript
Copy code
const numbers = [1, 2, 3, 4];
const doubled = numbers.map((n) => n * 2);
console.log(doubled); // [2, 4, 6, 8]

Use Cases

Transforming arrays (e.g., modifying data).
Mapping one format of data to another.

2. filter()

The filter() method creates a new array containing only the elements that satisfy a specified condition.

Syntax
javascript
Copy code
array.filter(callback(element, index, array), thisArg);

callback: A function that returns true or false for each element.

thisArg: (Optional) Value to use as this when executing the callback.

Example: Filtering Even Numbers

javascript
Copy code

```javascript
const numbers = [1, 2, 3, 4, 5];
const evenNumbers = numbers.filter((n) => n % 2 === 0);
console.log(evenNumbers); // [2, 4]
```

Use Cases

Filtering data based on conditions.
Removing unwanted or invalid data.

3. reduce()

The reduce() method applies a reducer function to each element of the array, resulting in a single output value.

Syntax

javascript
Copy code
array.reduce(callback(accumulator, currentValue, index, array), initialValue);

.

callback: A function that takes the accumulator and the current value.
initialValue: (Optional) Initial value for the accumulator.

Example: Summing Numbers

javascript
Copy code
```
const numbers = [1, 2, 3, 4];
const sum = numbers.reduce((total, num) => total + num, 0);
console.log(sum); // 10
```

Use Cases

Aggregating data (e.g., sum, product).
Transforming data structures (e.g., flattening arrays).

Combining map(), filter(), and reduce()

These methods can be chained together to perform complex operations in a concise and readable way.

Example: Calculate Total of Even Numbers Doubled

```javascript
Copy code
const numbers = [1, 2, 3, 4, 5, 6];
const result = numbers
  .filter((n) => n % 2 === 0)     // Filter even numbers: [2, 4, 6]
  .map((n) => n * 2)              // Double them: [4, 8, 12]
  .reduce((total, n) => total + n); // Sum: 24

console.log(result); // 24
```

Benefits of Using map(), filter(), and reduce()

Declarative Code: Improves readability by describing "what" to do, not "how" to do it.

Immutability: These methods do not modify the original array but return new ones.

Chaining: Easily combine these methods for complex operations.

Key Differences

Method	Purpose	Return Value
map()	Transforms each element.	A new array of the same length.
filter()	Filters elements based on a condition.	A new array with fewer or equal elements.
reduce()	Reduces elements to a single value	A single value (e.g., number, object).

Conclusion

The map(), filter(), and reduce() methods are essential tools in functional programming with JavaScript. They allow for clean, efficient, and declarative data processing, making code more readable and maintainable. By mastering these methods, developers can handle complex data transformations with ease.

4.2 Avoiding Side Effects

In functional programming, avoiding side effects is a fundamental principle. A side effect occurs when a function interacts with the outside world or modifies its external environment, such as altering global variables, modifying data structures, or performing I/O operations. Avoiding side effects leads to more predictable, testable, and maintainable code.

What Are Side Effects?

A side effect happens when a function:

Modifies a variable or object outside its own scope.
Interacts with external systems (e.g., file systems, databases, or APIs).

Produces observable changes beyond returning a value.

Example of a Function with Side Effects

javascript
Copy code
let counter = 0;

```
function increment() {
  counter += 1; // Modifies the external variable
    console.log(counter); // Logs to the console (I/O operation)
}
```

Why Avoid Side Effects?

Predictability: Pure functions (without side effects) always produce the same output for the same input.

Testability: Pure functions are easier to test because they don't depend on or alter external state.

Maintainability: Functions that don't cause side effects are easier to understand and debug.

Concurrency: Avoiding shared state prevents issues in concurrent or asynchronous environments.

How to Avoid Side Effects

Use Pure Functions

Ensure that a function's behavior is self-contained and doesn't depend on or alter external state.

```javascript
Copy code
function add(a, b) {
  return a + b; // No side effects
}
```

Avoid Mutating Data

Use immutability by creating new copies of data instead of modifying existing objects or arrays.

```javascript
Copy code
const array = [1, 2, 3];

// Avoid mutating the original array
const newArray = [...array, 4]; // [1, 2, 3, 4]
```

Minimize Global Variables

Keep variables local to functions or modules to reduce dependencies on external state.

javascript
Copy code
```
function calculateArea(radius) {
  return Math.PI * radius * radius; // Depends only on input
}
```

Use Functional Programming Techniques

Employ higher-order functions like map(), filter(), and reduce() for transformations.

javascript
Copy code
```
const numbers = [1, 2, 3, 4];
const doubled = numbers.map((n) => n * 2); // No side effects
```

Isolate Side Effects

If side effects are unavoidable (e.g., API calls, logging), isolate them in specific functions or layers of the application.

```javascript
Copy code
function logMessage(message) {
  console.log(message); // Side effect isolated here
}

function processData(data) {
  return data.map((item) => item * 2); // Pure function
}

const result = processData([1, 2, 3]);
logMessage(result); // Logging is external
```

Avoid Shared State

Prevent multiple functions from modifying the same data. Use closures or immutability to manage state.

```javascript
Copy code
function createCounter() {
  let count = 0;
```

```javascript
    return () => ++count; // Encapsulated state
}

const counter = createCounter();
console.log(counter()); // 1
console.log(counter()); // 2
```

Examples of Side Effects vs. Avoiding Them

Side Effects

```javascript
javascript
Copy code
let total = 0;

function addToTotal(value) {
    total += value; // Modifies external variable
    return total;
}

addToTotal(5);
console.log(total); // 5
```

Avoiding Side Effects

```javascript
Copy code
function add(a, b) {
  return a + b; // Pure function
}

const result = add(5, 10);
console.log(result); // 15
```

Benefits of Avoiding Side Effects

Reusable Code: Pure functions can be reused in different contexts without unintended consequences.

Simplified Debugging: Bugs are easier to isolate when functions don't alter external state.

Parallel Execution: Pure functions can be executed concurrently without conflicts.
Improved Performance: Immutable data structures reduce the risk of unintended modifications, ensuring stability.

Conclusion

Avoiding side effects is a core principle of functional programming. By using pure functions, maintaining immutability, and isolating unavoidable side effects, you can write predictable, maintainable, and robust JavaScript code. This approach not only simplifies debugging but also ensures better scalability and reliability in modern applications.

4.3 Recursion over Loops

In programming, recursion and loops are two fundamental techniques for iterating over data or performing repetitive tasks. While both approaches can often achieve the same result, recursion is favored in functional programming due to its elegant, declarative nature. Recursion involves a function calling itself, whereas loops use control flow structures (such as for, while, or do-while) to repeat code.

What is Recursion?

Recursion is a technique where a function calls itself in order to solve a problem. The key to recursion is having a base case—a condition that stops the recursion. Otherwise, the function will continue calling itself indefinitely.

Basic Structure of Recursion

Base Case: The condition that stops the recursion.
Recursive Case: The part of the function that calls itself with modified arguments.

Example of Recursion (Factorial)

The factorial of a number (denoted as n!) is the product of all positive integers less than or equal to n. The recursive approach to calculating the factorial is as follows:

```javascript
Copy code
function factorial(n) {
  if (n <= 1) {        // Base case
    return 1;
  } else {
    return n * factorial(n - 1); // Recursive case
  }
}

console.log(factorial(5)); // 120
```

Recursion vs. Loops

While recursion can be powerful, loops are often easier to understand for certain repetitive tasks. However, recursion can sometimes provide more elegant solutions, particularly when dealing with hierarchical data or problems that naturally fit the "divide and conquer" model.

Key Differences:

Feature	Recursion	Loops
Function Calls	The function calls itself, with a new set of arguments each time.	Uses an iterative structure to repeat a block of code.
Termination	Requires a base case to stop the recursion.	Automatically stops when the loop condition is false.
Memory Usage	Each recursive	Loops typically

	call adds to the call stack.	use less memory because they don't require additional stack frames.
Clarity	Recursion can be more elegant, especially for problems like tree traversal or divide-and-conq uer.	Loops can be simpler for straightforward iteration tasks.

Advantages of Recursion

Elegance: Recursion often leads to more concise and elegant solutions, especially when dealing with nested or hierarchical structures like trees or graphs.

Example: Sum of Nested Arrays (Flattening)

Recursion can be used to sum all numbers in an array, even if the array is nested:

javascript
Copy code

```javascript
function sumArray(arr) {
  return arr.reduce((acc, val) => {
    if (Array.isArray(val)) {
      return acc + sumArray(val);  // Recursive call for nested arrays
    } else {
      return acc + val;
    }
  }, 0);
}

console.log(sumArray([1, [2, 3], [4, [5, 6]]]));  // 21
```

Clarity in Complex Problems: Problems like tree traversal, factorial calculation, and
Fibonacci sequence can be written more naturally and clearly with recursion.

Decomposition: Recursion helps break down problems into smaller subproblems, which is useful in divide-and-conquer algorithms.

Disadvantages of Recursion

Performance Concerns: Each recursive call adds a new frame to the call stack. If the recursion depth is too large, it can lead to a stack overflow error.

Example of Stack Overflow

If a recursion has too many calls, it may exceed the JavaScript call stack:

```javascript
Copy code
function infiniteRecursion() {
  infiniteRecursion();
}

infiniteRecursion(); // Will throw a "
```

Maximum call stack size exceeded" error

Memory Consumption: Recursion can use more memory than loops due to the overhead of managing function calls and call stacks.

When to Use Recursion over Loops

Tree or Graph Traversals: Recursion is ideal for traversing hierarchical data structures like trees, where each node can have a variable number of children.

Example: Traversing a Binary Tree

```javascript
Copy code
function traverseTree(node) {
  if (!node) return;  // Base case: empty node
  console.log(node.value);
    traverseTree(node.left);   // Recursively traverse left
child
    traverseTree(node.right); // Recursively traverse right
child
}
```

Divide and Conquer Algorithms: Recursion is well-suited for problems that can be broken down into smaller, similar subproblems, like in quicksort or mergesort.

Mathematical Problems: Recursion is a natural fit for mathematical operations like calculating the factorial or the Fibonacci sequence.

Converting Recursion to Loops

For performance reasons, recursive solutions can often be converted into iterative ones. Using loops can avoid excessive function calls and reduce memory usage.

Example: Fibonacci Sequence

Recursive Approach:

```javascript
Copy code
function fibonacci(n) {
  if (n <= 1) return n;
  return fibonacci(n - 1) + fibonacci(n - 2);
}
console.log(fibonacci(6)); // 8
```

Iterative Approach:

javascript
Copy code
```javascript
function fibonacci(n) {
  let a = 0, b = 1;
  for (let i = 2; i <= n; i++) {
    const temp = a + b;
    a = b;
    b = temp;
  }
  return n === 0 ? a : b;
}

console.log(fibonacci(6)); // 8
```

Conclusion

Recursion and loops each have their strengths and weaknesses. Recursion is best suited for problems that require breaking down into smaller, similar subproblems or working with hierarchical data. On the other hand, loops are generally more efficient in terms of memory usage for straightforward iterative tasks. Choosing between the two depends on the nature of the problem at hand, performance considerations, and readability of the solution.

4.4 Currying and Partial Application

In functional programming, currying and partial application are two powerful techniques used to handle functions that take multiple arguments. Both methods allow for the creation of specialized versions of a function by pre-setting some of its arguments.

1. Currying

Currying is the process of transforming a function that takes multiple arguments into a series of functions, each taking a single argument. Instead of calling a function with all its arguments at once, curried functions can be invoked one argument at a time.

Key Characteristics of Currying

A curried function returns another function until all arguments are provided.
It allows you to create more specialized functions with fewer arguments.

Syntax of Currying

javascript
Copy code
```
function add(a) {
  return function(b) {
    return a + b;
  };
}

const add5 = add(5);  // Returns a function that adds 5 to its argument
console.log(add5(3)); // 8
```

Example: Currying a Simple Function

javascript
Copy code
```
function multiply(a) {
  return function(b) {
```

```javascript
    return a * b;
  };
}
```

```javascript
const double = multiply(2);   // Curried version of
multiply with 'a' set to 2
console.log(double(5)); // 10
```

Benefits of Currying

Reusability: You can create more specialized versions of a function.
Partial Application: Currying facilitates partial application by allowing some arguments to be pre-set.
Cleaner Code: Curried functions often lead to more concise and flexible code.

Currying with bind()

You can also curry functions using the bind() method, which pre-applies arguments:

javascript
Copy code

```javascript
const multiplyBy3 = multiply.bind(null, 3); // Currying using `bind`
console.log(multiplyBy3(4)); // 12
```

2. Partial Application

Partial application is the process of fixing a specific number of arguments to a function, producing a new function that takes the remaining arguments. Unlike currying, where functions are broken down into multiple single-argument functions, partial application allows you to apply some arguments upfront while leaving the rest to be passed later.

Key Characteristics of Partial Application

Partial application allows you to call a function with a subset of arguments, and it returns a new function that expects the remaining arguments.

It is different from currying because partial application doesn't always break down a function into single-argument functions, but it still allows pre-setting arguments.

Syntax of Partial Application
javascript

```javascript
function add(a, b, c) {
  return a + b + c;
}

function partial(fn, ...fixedArgs) {
  return function(...args) {
    return fn(...fixedArgs, ...args);
  };
}

const add5And10 = partial(add, 5, 10);
console.log(add5And10(15)); // 30
```

Example: Partial Application

javascript

```javascript
function greet(greeting, name) {
  return `${greeting}, ${name}!`;
}

const sayHello = greet.bind(null, 'Hello'); // Partial application with 'Hello' fixed
console.log(sayHello('Alice')); // "Hello, Alice!"
```

Benefits of Partial Application

Code Reusability: Create new functions by applying some arguments, reducing code duplication.

Flexibility: You can delay the passing of some arguments while fixing others.

Improved Readability: By creating more specialized functions, you can improve the clarity and intent of your code.

Difference Between Currying and Partial Application

Aspect	Currying	Partial Application
Function Type	Transforms a function into a series of unary (single-argument) functions.	Pre-applies some arguments to a function and returns a new function.
Arguments Handling	Each function accepts	Some arguments are fixed, and

	only one argument.	others can be passed later
Example Use Case	Calculating multiply(a)(b) where a and b are handled one at a time.	Pre-setting specific configuration values, like greet("Hello", "John") becomes greet("Hello").
Purpose	To transform multi-argument functions into a chain of single-argument functions.	To fix some arguments in advance, making a new function with fewer arguments to pass.

.

Combining Currying and Partial Application

You can combine currying and partial application to create very flexible and reusable functions.

Example: Combining Both

javascript
Copy code

```javascript
function multiply(a) {
  return function(b) {
    return a * b;
  };
}

function partial(fn, ...fixedArgs) {
  return function(...args) {
    return fn(...fixedArgs, ...args);
  };
}

const multiplyBy2 = partial(multiply(2));   // Partial application with 2 fixed
console.log(multiplyBy2(5)); // 10
```

In this example, the multiply function is curried to take one argument at a time, and then partial application allows us to pre-set 2 as one of the arguments.

Conclusion

Currying and partial application are two key techniques in functional programming that enable you to handle functions more flexibly and efficiently.

Currying allows you to break down functions into a series of functions that take one argument at a time, making it easier to create reusable, specialized functions.

Partial application enables you to fix some arguments of a function upfront, returning a new function that takes the remaining arguments.

By understanding and leveraging these techniques, you can write cleaner, more modular code that is easier to maintain and extend.

Chapter 5
Libraries for Functional Programming

In JavaScript, there are several libraries that help implement functional programming principles, providing utilities to make functional techniques like currying, immutability, higher-order functions, and more, easier to work with. These libraries enable developers to write cleaner, more declarative, and maintainable code using functional programming patterns.

Here are some of the most popular libraries for functional programming in JavaScript:

1. Lodash/Fp

Lodash is one of the most widely used utility libraries in JavaScript, offering a wide range of functions for manipulating arrays, objects, strings, and more. The lodash/fp module is the functional programming version of Lodash, which provides a more functional approach to working with the library's functions, including curried functions and immutable data handling.

Key Features:

Curried functions for a functional style.
Immutable methods that avoid side effects.
Higher-order functions like map, filter, and reduce.

Example:

javascript

```
Copy code
const _ = require('lodash/fp');

const add = (a, b) => a + b;
const curriedAdd = _.curry(add);

const result = curriedAdd(1)(2); // 3
```

2. Ramda

Ramda is a purely functional programming library for JavaScript. Unlike Lodash, which is designed for both imperative and functional styles, Ramda is built specifically to support a functional style. It emphasizes immutability, point-free functions, and currying out of the box.

Key Features:

Functions are curried by default.
Emphasis on immutability and side-effect-free functions.
Supports point-free style, where functions are composed without referring to arguments directly.

Example:

```javascript
Copy code
const R = require('ramda');

const add = (a, b) => a + b;
const curriedAdd = R.curry(add);

const result = curriedAdd(1)(2);  // 3
```

3. Immutable.js

Immutable.js provides persistent data structures that allow for functional programming with immutable data. This library is useful when you want to avoid modifying data directly and instead work with efficient, immutable data structures.

Key Features:

Persistent data structures like lists, maps, and sets.
Immutable collections ensure that data can't be changed directly.
Efficient methods for updating collections without mutations.

Example:

```javascript
Copy code
const { List } = require('immutable');

const list1 = List([1, 2, 3]);
const list2 = list1.push(4); // Returns a new list

console.log(list1); // List [1, 2, 3]
console.log(list2); // List [1, 2, 3, 4]
```

4. Folktale

Folktale is a functional programming library that provides a wide range of functional data structures and helpers for JavaScript, including Maybe, Result, Validation, and other functional abstractions. It's designed for developers who want to write functional code with an emphasis on error handling and data manipulation.

Key Features:

Includes algebraic data types such as Maybe, Result, and Validation.

Provides utilities for composing functions and handling errors without throwing exceptions.
Designed to integrate well with other functional libraries and frameworks.

Example:

```javascript
Copy code
const { Maybe } = require('folktale/maybe');

const findUser = (id) => {
  return id === 1 ? Maybe.Just({ name: 'John' }) : Maybe.Nothing();
};

const user = findUser(1);
console.log(user.getOrElse('User not found'));   // { name: 'John' }
```

5. Ramda Fantasy

Ramda Fantasy extends the Ramda library with more advanced functional programming tools. It includes additional monads, such as Maybe, Either, and IO, for building functional applications that handle errors, state, and computations in a more declarative way.

Key Features:

Provides more functional constructs like monads, functors, and applicatives.

Includes algebraic data types like Maybe, Either, and IO to handle computations and side effects safely.

Works well alongside Ramda for a more comprehensive functional approach.

Example:

javascript
Copy code

```javascript
const { Maybe } = require('ramda-fantasy');

const safeDiv = (x, y) => y === 0 ? Maybe.Nothing() : Maybe.Just(x / y);

const result = safeDiv(10, 2);
console.log(result.getOrElse('Cannot divide')); // 5
```

6. Sanctuary

Sanctuary is a library for functional programming in JavaScript that offers a strong focus on immutability, purity, and type safety. It provides a robust set of functional programming utilities and ensures type correctness using JavaScript's type system.

Key Features:

Strong type safety with types that are statically enforced.
Includes common functional programming tools like map, chain, and reduce.
Immutable data structures that prevent side effects and state mutations.

Example:

```javascript
Copy code
const S = require('sanctuary');

const add = (a, b) => a + b;
```

```
const curriedAdd = S.curry(add);
const result = curriedAdd(1)(2); // 3
```

Conclusion

These libraries make it easier to adopt functional programming patterns in JavaScript and provide a robust set of tools for working with functions, immutability, higher-order functions, and more. Whether you're looking for better ways to handle immutability, work with curried functions, or manage errors functionally, these libraries offer well-tested solutions that can improve the clarity, maintainability, and scalability of your code. By incorporating these functional programming libraries into your workflow, you can create cleaner, more efficient, and declarative JavaScript code.

5.1 Introduction to Lodash and Ramda

Both Lodash and Ramda are powerful utility libraries in JavaScript that help developers write cleaner, more efficient, and readable code. However, they approach functional programming from different perspectives. Lodash is a versatile utility library, while Ramda is designed specifically for functional programming, offering a functional and immutable approach to handling data and functions.

Let's dive into a brief introduction of both libraries.

1. Lodash
Lodash is one of the most popular utility libraries in JavaScript, providing a wide range of functions to simplify common programming tasks. It focuses on offering performance optimizations and easy-to-use methods for manipulating arrays, objects, strings, and other data types.

Key Features of Lodash:

Utility Functions: Lodash provides a rich set of functions that help with common operations like deep cloning objects, merging arrays, filtering collections, etc.

Modular Design: Lodash is modular, meaning that you can import only the functions you need, reducing the size of your application.

Performance: Lodash is optimized for speed, often outperforming the native JavaScript equivalents, especially in complex operations.

Cross-Browser Compatibility: Lodash works across different browsers, ensuring that your code works seamlessly in various environments.

Example of Using Lodash:

```javascript
Copy code
const _ = require('lodash');

// Working with arrays
const array = [1, 2, 3, 4, 5];
const chunked = _.chunk(array, 2); // Splits array into smaller chunks
console.log(chunked); // [[1, 2], [3, 4], [5]]

// Cloning objects
```

```
const object = { name: 'John', age: 30 };
const clonedObject = _.cloneDeep(object);
console.log(clonedObject);  // { name: 'John', age: 30 }
```

Usage in Functional Programming:

Although Lodash can be used in both imperative and functional programming styles, the lodash/fp module focuses on curried and immutable versions of Lodash's functions, making it a better fit for functional programming.

2. Ramda

Ramda is a functional programming library designed specifically for JavaScript. It emphasizes a purely functional approach, offering immutable data structures, curried functions by default, and tools for composing and manipulating functions.

Key Features of Ramda:

Curried by Default: All functions in Ramda are curried by default, which means they can be called with one argument at a time, allowing for better composability and reuse.

Immutable: Ramda focuses on immutability, ensuring that functions don't mutate the input data.

Point-Free Style: Ramda supports point-free programming, where functions are composed without referencing the arguments explicitly.

Function Composition: It provides easy-to-use utilities like compose and pipe for composing and chaining functions.

Example of Using Ramda:

javascript
Copy code
```javascript
const R = require('ramda');

// Currying and composition
const add = (a, b) => a + b;
const curriedAdd = R.curry(add);

const result = curriedAdd(5)(10); // 15
console.log(result);

// Composing functions
```

```
const greet = (name) => `Hello, ${name}`;
const exclaim = (greeting) => `${greeting}!`;

const greetAndExclaim = R.compose(exclaim, greet);
console.log(greetAndExclaim('Alice'));        //    "Hello,
Alice!"
```

Functional Programming in Ramda:

Currying: Functions can be curried automatically, which simplifies the composition of functions.

Immutability: Operations with data structures are designed to avoid mutating original data.

Function Composition: Functions are easily composed using compose and pipe to create pipelines of transformations.

Lodash vs. Ramda

Feature	Lodash	Ramda
Style	Supports both functional and imperative styles.	Designed specifically for functional programming.
Currying	Optional, using the lodash/fp module	Functions are curried by default.
Immutability	Lodash does not emphasize immutability by default.	Strong emphasis on immutability.
Composition	Provides some basic composition tools (e.g., _.flow), but not as central.	Functions like compose and pipe are central for composition.
Utility Functions	Comprehensive set of utilities for arrays, objects, and more.	Focused on functional utilities, like composition,

		currying, and immutability.

.

When to Use Lodash or Ramda?

Lodash is ideal when you need a general-purpose utility library with a wide variety of functions to simplify your code. It's perfect for quick, performance-optimized solutions to common tasks like manipulating arrays and objects. If you prefer a more imperative approach or need to work with both functional and non-functional styles, Lodash is a great choice.

Ramda is better suited for developers who are working with a functional programming paradigm. Its currying, composition tools, and immutability features make it a good choice when building applications that emphasize pure functions, immutability, and function composition.

Conclusion

Both Lodash and Ramda are powerful libraries, but they cater to different needs and approaches to programming. Lodash is a versatile utility library for a variety of programming styles, while Ramda is a dedicated functional programming library that encourages a more declarative and functional approach to JavaScript. Depending on the requirements of your project and your preferred coding style, you can choose the one that best fits your needs or even use both in combination for maximum flexibility.

5.2 Key Functions and Use Cases

Functional programming in JavaScript relies on key functions and techniques to create modular, efficient, and declarative code. These functions simplify data manipulation, enhance code readability, and enable better reuse. Here's an overview of key functions and their use cases in functional programming, primarily focusing on built-in JavaScript methods and utilities provided by libraries like Lodash and Ramda.

1. map()

Description: Transforms each element in a collection (array or object) by applying a provided function.

Use Case: Used to create a new array with elements transformed based on specific logic.

Example:

```javascript
Copy code
const numbers = [1, 2, 3, 4];
const doubled = numbers.map((n) => n * 2);
console.log(doubled); // [2, 4, 6, 8]
```

2. filter()

Description: Filters elements from a collection based on a condition (predicate function).

Use Case: Useful for removing unwanted data or extracting subsets of data.

Example:

javascript
Copy code
```
const numbers = [1, 2, 3, 4];
const evenNumbers = numbers.filter((n) => n % 2 === 0);
console.log(evenNumbers); // [2, 4]
```

3. reduce()

Description: Reduces a collection to a single value by applying a function iteratively to each element and an accumulator.
Use Case: Ideal for summing numbers, flattening arrays, or aggregating data into objects.

Example:

javascript
Copy code
```
const numbers = [1, 2, 3, 4];
const sum = numbers.reduce((acc, n) => acc + n, 0);
console.log(sum); // 10
```

4. forEach()

Description: Iterates over a collection, executing a provided function for each element.
Use Case: Useful for performing side effects like logging or making API calls.

Example:

```javascript
Copy code
const fruits = ['apple', 'banana', 'cherry'];
fruits.forEach((fruit) => console.log(fruit));
// Output:
// apple
// banana
// cherry
```

5. Function Composition (compose() and pipe())

Description: Combines multiple functions into a pipeline to transform data step by step.

Use Case: Used to create readable and reusable workflows.

Example:

javascript
Copy code

```
const R = require('ramda');
const double = (x) => x * 2;
const subtractOne = (x) => x - 1;
const transform = R.compose(double, subtractOne); // Right-to-left
console.log(transform(5)); // 8
```

6. curry()

Description: Converts a function so it can be called with fewer arguments than it expects, returning a new function for the remaining arguments.

Use Case: Useful for creating reusable, partially applied functions.

Example:

javascript
Copy code

```
const R = require('ramda');
const add = (a, b) => a + b;
const curriedAdd = R.curry(add);
console.log(curriedAdd(5)(10)); // 15
```

7. debounce() and throttle() (from Lodash)

Description:

debounce(): Delays a function until after a specified time has passed since the last call.

throttle(): Ensures a function is called at most once in a specified time frame.

Use Case: Commonly used for optimizing events like resizing or scrolling.

Example:

javascript
Copy code
```
const _ = require('lodash');
const log = _.debounce(() => console.log('Resized!'), 300);
window.addEventListener('resize', log);
```

8. cloneDeep() (from Lodash)

Description: Creates a deep copy of a value, including nested structures.
Use Case: Prevents unintended mutations by ensuring the original object is not affected.

Example:

javascript
Copy code
```
const _ = require('lodash');
const obj = { a: 1, b: { c: 2 } };
const clonedObj = _.cloneDeep(obj);
clonedObj.b.c = 3;
console.log(obj.b.c); // 2
```

9. groupBy() (from Lodash)

Description: Groups elements of a collection based on a key or function.

Use Case: Useful for categorizing data.

Example:

```javascript
Copy code
const _ = require('lodash');
const users = [
  { name: 'Alice', age: 25 },
  { name: 'Bob', age: 30 },
  { name: 'Charlie', age: 25 },
];
const grouped = _.groupBy(users, 'age');
console.log(grouped);
// { 25: [{ name: 'Alice' }, { name: 'Charlie' }], 30: [{ name: 'Bob' }] }
```

10. pick() and omit() (from Lodash)

Description:

pick(): Creates an object with specified keys from an original object.
omit(): Excludes specified keys from an object.
Use Case: Useful for selecting or excluding fields from data objects.

Example:

javascript
Copy code
```
const _ = require('lodash');
const obj = { a: 1, b: 2, c: 3 };
const picked = _.pick(obj, ['a', 'c']);
console.log(picked); // { a: 1, c: 3 }
```

11. R.path() and R.assoc() (from Ramda)

Description:

R.path(): Safely retrieves a nested property from an object.
R.assoc(): Creates a new object by updating a specific key.
Use Case: Ideal for working with nested data in immutable structures.

Example:

javascript
Copy code
```
const R = require('ramda');
const obj = { a: { b: { c: 42 } } };
```

```
const value = R.path(['a', 'b', 'c'], obj);
console.log(value); // 42

const updated = R.assoc('d', 100, obj);
console.log(updated); // { a: { b: { c: 42 } }, d: 100 }
```

12. Immutability Utilities

Description: Functions like Object.freeze() and libraries like Immutable.js ensure data cannot be mutated.
Use Case: Used to maintain predictable state in functional programming.

Example:

```javascript
Copy code
const obj = Object.freeze({ a: 1, b: 2 });
obj.a = 2; // Error: Cannot assign to read-only property
```

Conclusion

These key functions and their use cases form the foundation of functional programming in JavaScript. By leveraging built-in methods and external libraries like Lodash and Ramda, developers can write cleaner, more modular, and efficient code while adhering to functional programming principles such as immutability, pure functions, and declarative logic.

5.3 Choosing the Right Library

When incorporating functional programming into your JavaScript projects, you have several libraries at your disposal to simplify and enhance your code. Two of the most popular libraries are Lodash and Ramda, both of which provide powerful utilities for functional programming. However, choosing the right library for your project depends on several factors, such as the complexity of your use case, performance considerations, and your team's familiarity with functional programming concepts.

Here's a guide to help you choose the right functional programming library based on your project needs.

1. Lodash
Overview

Lodash is a utility library that provides a wide variety of functions to work with arrays, objects, and other data structures. While Lodash is not specifically built for functional programming, it does offer functional programming features through its lodash/fp module, which allows you to work with curried functions and immutable data.

When to Choose Lodash

General Utility Needs: If your project requires a wide range of utilities beyond functional programming (e.g., deep cloning, object merging, and array manipulation), Lodash is an excellent choice. It is a mature and widely-used library with comprehensive functionality.

Performance Sensitivity: Lodash is highly optimized for performance, making it suitable for large-scale applications where performance is critical.

Legacy Projects: If you are working with a legacy codebase or a team that is not yet familiar with functional programming, Lodash's simplicity and broad usage make it easier to adopt without a steep learning curve.

Interoperability with Imperative Code: If you are gradually transitioning an existing imperative codebase to functional programming, Lodash allows you to integrate functional programming features without having to refactor the entire codebase.

Example Use Case

Working with arrays or objects where you need utilities like map, filter, reduce, cloneDeep, merge, or debounce. Lodash's wide range of functions makes it a good all-rounder when functional programming is not the sole focus of the project.

Example Code:

```javascript
Copy code
const _ = require('lodash');
```

```
const users = [
  { name: 'Alice', age: 25 },
  { name: 'Bob', age: 30 },
  { name: 'Charlie', age: 25 }
];

// Group users by age
const grouped = _.groupBy(users, 'age');
console.log(grouped);
// Output: { 25: [{ name: 'Alice' }, { name: 'Charlie' }],
30: [{ name: 'Bob' }] }
```

2. Ramda

Overview

Ramda is a library specifically built for functional programming in JavaScript. It embraces immutability and currying by default, offering a wide range of pure functions that work seamlessly with JavaScript's functional programming paradigm. Ramda is designed to be fully functional, with no side effects or mutations.

When to Choose Ramda

Full Functional Programming Approach: If your project is fully embracing functional programming principles, Ramda is a better fit. Its functions are curried by default, making them more composable and suited for declarative code.

Immutability and Side Effect-Free Operations: Ramda's approach ensures that all operations are immutable and that data is never mutated. This is useful in situations where state management and avoiding side effects are crucial.

Function Composition and Currying: If you need to create pipelines of transformations and work extensively with curried functions, Ramda's built-in compose() and pipe() functions are incredibly powerful.

Declarative Style: Ramda's API is built for a declarative programming style, making it easy to express complex operations in a concise and readable way.

Example Use Case

Building a functional pipeline where operations are combined step-by-step. Ramda's currying, function composition, and higher-order functions make it ideal for writing clean, functional code in complex applications where immutability is required.

Example Code:

javascript
Copy code
```javascript
const R = require('ramda');
const double = (x) => x * 2;
const subtractOne = (x) => x - 1;
const process = R.compose(subtractOne, double);
```

console.log(process(5)); // 9 (First doubles 5 to get 10, then subtracts 1 to get 9)

3. When to Use Both Together

In some projects, it may be beneficial to combine Lodash and Ramda. While Ramda is great for pure functional programming, Lodash provides additional utility functions that are not focused on functional programming but are highly practical in general programming tasks (like deep cloning, merging objects, and working with collections). Using both libraries together can allow you to get the best of both worlds: functional programming from Ramda and utility functions from Lodash.

4. Key Differences to Consider

Immutability: Ramda enforces immutability, whereas Lodash (outside of lodash/fp) allows mutable operations. If immutability is a core principle in your project, Ramda is a better fit.

Currying: Ramda functions are curried by default, which makes it easier to compose and partially apply functions. Lodash's functions need to be explicitly curried if you use the lodash/fp version.

Function Composition: Ramda's compose and pipe functions are powerful tools for function composition. Lodash's flow (or _.flow) works similarly but does not have the same focus on immutability and pure functions.

Learning Curve: Lodash is simpler to pick up for those who are not familiar with functional programming, while Ramda requires a stronger understanding of functional concepts like currying and function composition.

5. Performance Considerations

Lodash: Lodash is highly optimized for performance and is suitable for performance-sensitive applications, especially when dealing with large data sets or when frequent utility function calls are involved.

Ramda: While Ramda is designed for functional programming, its performance may not be as optimized as Lodash, especially when dealing with large-scale data manipulation tasks. However, for most use cases that focus on immutability and composition, the performance difference is negligible.

Conclusion: Choosing the Right Library

Choose Lodash if your project requires a mix of utility functions, you need performance optimizations, or if you are working on an existing non-functional codebase where you want to gradually introduce functional programming concepts.

Choose Ramda if you are focused on full functional programming, need function composition, curried functions, and want to ensure immutability and avoid side effects.

Combine Both when you need a comprehensive set of utilities and are building a project that balances functional programming with general utility functions.

By considering your project's requirements, team expertise, and functional programming goals, you can make an informed choice between Lodash and Ramda—or decide to use both to maximize flexibility.

Chapter 6
Advanced Functional Programming

Advanced functional programming in JavaScript involves leveraging complex concepts and techniques to build robust, reusable, and highly maintainable code. These advanced topics go beyond the basics of pure functions, immutability, and higher-order functions, diving deeper into paradigms that promote declarative and expressive programming.

Key Concepts of Advanced Functional Programming

1. Currying and Partial Application
Currying: Breaking down a function that takes multiple arguments into a sequence of functions that each take a single argument.
Partial Application: Pre-filling some arguments of a function, creating a new function with fewer parameters.

Use Case: Enhances reusability and composability in code.

Example:

javascript

Copy code

```
const add = (a) => (b) => a + b;
const addFive = add(5);
console.log(addFive(10)); // 15
```

2. Function Composition

Definition: Combining multiple functions to create a new function, where the output of one function becomes the input of the next.

Use Case: Simplifies complex transformations and promotes code reuse.

Example:

javascript

Copy code

```
const R = require('ramda');
const double = (x) => x * 2;
const increment = (x) => x + 1;
const process = R.compose(double, increment);
```

console.log(process(3)); // 8

3. Monads

Definition: A design pattern that helps manage side effects and asynchronous operations, often used with promises or functional data structures.

Use Case: Ensures predictable behavior in workflows involving side effects.

Example:

javascript
Copy code
```
Promise.resolve(5)
  .then((x) => x * 2)
  .then((x) => x + 3)
  .then(console.log); // 13
```

4. Lazy Evaluation

Definition: Delaying the computation of a value until it is actually needed.

Use Case: Improves performance by avoiding unnecessary computations, particularly in large datasets.

Example:

javascript
Copy code
const lazyMap = (arr, fn) => arr.map(() => fn);

5. Functional Reactive Programming (FRP)

Definition: Combines functional programming with reactive data streams, often implemented using libraries like RxJS.

Use Case: Handles asynchronous data streams, such as user inputs or real-time updates.

Example:

javascript
Copy code
const { fromEvent } = require('rxjs');
fromEvent(document,   'click').subscribe(()   =>
console.log('Clicked!'));

6. Point-Free Style

Definition: Writing functions without explicitly mentioning their arguments, focusing instead on the composition of operations.

Use Case: Makes code more concise and expressive.

Example:

```javascript
Copy code
const R = require('ramda');
const toUpperCase = R.toUpper;
const greet = R.compose(toUpperCase, (name) => `Hello, ${name}`);
console.log(greet('Alice')); // HELLO, ALICE
```

Benefits of Advanced Functional Programming

Promotes reusability and modularity.
Simplifies complex logic using declarative patterns.

Enhances maintainability by avoiding side effects and enforcing immutability.

Enables parallelization and asynchronous processing in clean workflows.

Advanced functional programming unlocks the true potential of JavaScript, enabling developers to build scalable and efficient applications by adhering to principles of immutability, pure functions, and declarative logic.

6.1 Closures and Their Applications

What is a Closure?

A closure is a function that "remembers" the variables from its lexical scope even after the outer function has executed. Closures are created every time a function is defined, allowing the function to access variables from its outer scope.

How Closures Work

Closures are enabled by the way JavaScript handles scopes and execution contexts.

When a function is returned or passed as an argument, it retains access to the variables that were in scope at the time it was created.

Syntax Example

```javascript
Copy code
function outerFunction(outerVariable) {
  return function innerFunction(innerVariable) {
    console.log(`Outer Variable: ${outerVariable}, Inner Variable: ${innerVariable}`);
  };
}


const closureExample = outerFunction('outside');
closureExample('inside');
// Output: Outer Variable: outside, Inner Variable: inside
```

Applications of Closures

1. Data Privacy and Encapsulation

Closures are often used to create private variables in JavaScript, providing a way to encapsulate data and prevent direct access.

Example:

```javascript
Copy code
function counter() {
  let count = 0;
  return {
    increment: () => ++count,
    decrement: () => --count,
    getCount: () => count,
  };
}

const myCounter = counter();
console.log(myCounter.increment()); // 1
console.log(myCounter.decrement()); // 0
console.log(myCounter.getCount());  // 0
```

2. Function Factories

Closures can be used to create reusable function factories that generate functions tailored to specific use cases.

Example:

```javascript
Copy code
function multiplier(factor) {
  return function (number) {
    return number * factor;
  };
}


const double = multiplier(2);
const triple = multiplier(3);


console.log(double(5)); // 10
console.log(triple(5)); // 15
```

3. Maintaining State

Closures allow you to maintain a state in functions without relying on global variables.

Example:

```javascript
Copy code
function statefulAdder(initialValue) {
  let value = initialValue;
  return (increment) => {
    value += increment;
    return value;
  };
}

const add = statefulAdder(10);
console.log(add(5)); // 15
console.log(add(10)); // 25
```

4. Event Handlers

Closures are commonly used in event listeners, where the handler function "remembers" the variables it had access to when it was created.

Example:

javascript

```
Copy code
function createClickHandler(message) {
  return function () {
    console.log(message);
  };
}


const button = document.createElement('button');
button.textContent = 'Click Me';
button.addEventListener('click',
createClickHandler('Button Clicked!'));
document.body.appendChild(button);
```

5. Iterators and Generators

Closures can be used to implement custom iterators and generators that "remember" their current state.

Example:

```javascript
Copy code
function createIterator(array) {
  let index = 0;
  return function () {
```

```
    return index < array.length ? array[index++] :
undefined;
  };
}


const next = createIterator([1, 2, 3]);
console.log(next()); // 1
console.log(next()); // 2
console.log(next()); // 3
console.log(next()); // undefined
```

6. Memoization

Closures are useful for memoizing expensive computations
by storing results in a closure-scoped cache.

Example:

javascript
Copy code
```
function memoize(fn) {
  const cache = {};
  return function (arg) {
    if (cache[arg]) {
      console.log('Fetching from cache');
```

```
    return cache[arg];
  }
  console.log('Calculating result');
  const result = fn(arg);
  cache[arg] = result;
  return result;
 };
}
```

```
const square = memoize((x) => x * x);
console.log(square(4)); // Calculating result, 16
console.log(square(4)); // Fetching from cache, 16
```

7. Asynchronous Programming

.

Closures enable callback functions to access variables in their outer scope, making them crucial in asynchronous programming.

Example:

javascript
Copy code
```
function delayedGreeting(name) {
  setTimeout(() => {
```

```
    console.log(`Hello, ${name}!`);
  }, 1000);
}


delayedGreeting('Alice');
// Output (after 1 second): Hello, Alice!
```

Advantages of Closures

Data security: Protects variables from being accessed or modified directly.
State management: Enables functions to maintain their state across multiple calls.
Modularity: Encourages reusable and composable code.

Conclusion

Closures are a powerful feature of JavaScript, providing a way to create private variables, manage state, and enable advanced programming techniques. They are widely used in real-world applications such as event handling, asynchronous operations, and functional programming, making them an essential concept for JavaScript developers.

6.2 Functional Composition with pipe() and compose()

Functional composition is a technique in functional programming where multiple functions are combined to create a new function. This approach enables developers to structure programs in a clean, declarative manner, making code more modular and easier to understand.

In JavaScript, libraries like Ramda and lodash/fp provide utilities such as pipe() and compose() for functional composition. These tools allow functions to be chained together seamlessly.

Understanding compose()

compose() creates a new function by combining multiple functions in a right-to-left order. The output of one function becomes the input for the next function in the chain, starting from the rightmost function.

Syntax:

javascript

Copy code

compose(fn1, fn2, fn3)(value);

// Equivalent to: fn1(fn2(fn3(value)));

Example:

javascript

Copy code

const R = require('ramda');

const toUpperCase = (str) => str.toUpperCase();

const exclaim = (str) => `${str}!`;

const shout = R.compose(exclaim, toUpperCase);

console.log(shout('hello')); // Output: HELLO!

Understanding pipe()

pipe() works similarly to compose() but processes functions in a left-to-right order. It is often preferred when the flow of data mirrors the natural sequence of operations.

Syntax:

javascript
Copy code
pipe(fn1, fn2, fn3)(value);
// Equivalent to: fn3(fn2(fn1(value)));

Example:

javascript
Copy code
const R = require('ramda');
const add = (x) => x + 1;
const double = (x) => x * 2;
const processNumber = R.pipe(add, double);

console.log(processNumber(5)); // Output: 12 (5 + 1 =
6, then 6 * 2 = 12)

Key Differences Between pipe() and compose()

Feature	compose()	pipe()

Order	Right-to-left	Left-to-right
Readability	Best for reverse-order logic	Easier to read for sequential logic
Common Usage	Mathematically inclined operations	Natural workflows or transformations

Applications of pipe() and compose()

1. Data Transformation

These functions are ideal for transforming data through a series of operations.

Example:

javascript

```
Copy code
const sanitizeInput = (str) => str.trim();
const toLowerCase = (str) => str.toLowerCase();
const formatInput = R.pipe(sanitizeInput,
toLowerCase);

console.log(formatInput('  Hello World  ')); // Output:
"hello world"
```

2. Building Reusable Pipelines

Functional composition allows you to build reusable
pipelines for repetitive tasks.

Example:

javascript
```
Copy code
const calculateDiscount = (price) => price * 0.9;
const formatCurrency = (price) =>
`$${price.toFixed(2)}`;
const processPrice = R.pipe(calculateDiscount,
formatCurrency);

console.log(processPrice(100)); // Output: "$90.00"
```

3. Reducing Complexity

Composing functions reduces the complexity of nested function calls and makes code easier to debug.

Without Composition:

javascript
Copy code
```
const result = exclaim(toUpperCase('hello'));
console.log(result); // HELLO!
```

With Composition:

javascript
Copy code
```
const shout = R.compose(exclaim, toUpperCase);
console.log(shout('hello')); // HELLO!
```

4. Functional Data Flow

pipe() and compose() are invaluable when designing functional data flows, especially in frameworks or libraries like Redux, where transformations occur in sequence.

Example:

```javascript
Copy code
const addTax = (price) => price * 1.1;
const applyCoupon = (price) => price - 5;
const calculateFinalPrice = R.pipe(addTax, applyCoupon);

console.log(calculateFinalPrice(100)); // Output: 105
```

Benefits of Using pipe() and compose()

Improved Readability: Simplifies complex operations by chaining them declaratively.

Modularity: Promotes reusable and testable functions.

Avoids Nested Calls: Eliminates deeply nested function calls, reducing cognitive load.

Declarative Syntax: Encourages a functional programming style that is more intuitive and predictable.

When to Use pipe() or compose()

Use pipe() when the sequence of operations flows naturally from start to end, matching the logical progression of data. Use compose() when you prefer working in reverse order, especially in mathematical or theoretical applications.

Conclusion

pipe() and compose() are essential tools for functional programming in JavaScript. By enabling clean, modular, and declarative code, they help developers manage complex operations efficiently. Whether you choose pipe() for left-to-right clarity or compose() for mathematical elegance, both tools enhance the readability and maintainability of your codebase.

6.3 Lazy Evaluation

Lazy evaluation is a programming technique where expressions are not immediately evaluated but are deferred until their results are needed. This approach optimizes performance by avoiding unnecessary computations and memory usage, particularly in scenarios involving large datasets or expensive operations.

In JavaScript, lazy evaluation can be implemented manually or through libraries like Lodash, Ramda, or Lazy.js. Although JavaScript is not inherently lazy, its functional programming capabilities allow for lazy-like behavior.

Key Features of Lazy Evaluation

Deferred Execution

Computations are postponed until their results are explicitly requested.

Improved Performance

Avoids unnecessary computations, reducing resource consumption.

Efficiency with Infinite Data

Handles infinite or large datasets without running out of memory.

Composability

Works well with functional programming paradigms to build modular pipelines.

How Lazy Evaluation Works

Lazy evaluation often uses techniques like closures, generators, or streams to defer computation. Instead of producing a complete result immediately, it produces values on demand.

Example Using Generators

Generators are an excellent way to achieve lazy evaluation in JavaScript.

```javascript
Copy code
function* lazyRange(start, end) {
  for (let i = start; i < end; i++) {
    yield i;
  }
}
```

```
const numbers = lazyRange(1, 5);
console.log(numbers.next().value); // 1
console.log(numbers.next().value); // 2
console.log(numbers.next().value); // 3
```

Here, the range is computed lazily. Values are generated only when next() is called.

Benefits of Lazy Evaluation

Memory Efficiency

Only the required part of a dataset is loaded or computed, saving memory.

Performance Optimization

Reduces computation time by skipping unnecessary operations.

Scalability

Handles large datasets or infinite streams without crashing the program.

Composable Pipelines

Enables chaining of operations without evaluating the intermediate results until needed.

Applications of Lazy Evaluation

1. Infinite Data Streams

Lazy evaluation allows the creation of infinite sequences without exhausting resources.

Example:

```javascript
Copy code
function* infiniteSequence() {
  let i = 0;
  while (true) {
    yield i++;
  }
}

const sequence = infiniteSequence();
console.log(sequence.next().value); // 0
console.log(sequence.next().value); // 1
```

2. Lazy Data Processing

Used for optimizing operations on large datasets, such as filtering and mapping, without loading everything into memory.

Example:

```javascript
Copy code
function* lazyFilter(array, predicate) {
  for (const item of array) {
    if (predicate(item)) {
      yield item;
    }
  }
}

const numbers = [1, 2, 3, 4, 5];
const evenNumbers = lazyFilter(numbers, (x) => x % 2 === 0);

console.log([...evenNumbers]); // [2, 4]
```

3. Paginated or Streamed APIs

Lazy evaluation is used in APIs to load only the required data when interacting with large datasets.

4. Avoiding Expensive Computations

Lazy evaluation defers complex computations until absolutely necessary.

Example:

javascript
Copy code
```
const lazySquare = (x) => () => x * x;

const computeSquare = lazySquare(5);
console.log("Before computation");
console.log(computeSquare()); // Now computes 25
```

Libraries for Lazy Evaluation

1. Lazy.js

Lazy.js is a utility library for working with lazy sequences.

Example:

```javascript
Copy code
const Lazy = require('lazy.js');
const result = Lazy([1, 2, 3, 4])
  .filter((x) => x % 2 === 0)
  .map((x) => x * x)
  .toArray();

console.log(result); // [4, 16]
```

2. Lodash

Lodash supports lazy evaluation for chaining operations.

Example:

```javascript
Copy code
const _ = require('lodash');
const result = _(Array.from({ length: 1000 }))
  .filter((x) => x % 2 === 0)
  .map((x) => x * x)
```

```
.take(5)
.value();
```

```
console.log(result);
```

Lazy Evaluation vs. Eager Evaluation

Feature	Lazy Evaluation	Eager Evaluation
Execution Timing	Deferred until needed Immediate	Memory Usage Efficient, processes data in chunks Consumes more memory upfront
Performance	Skips unnecessary computations	Executes all operations eagerly
Applicability	Ideal for large/infinite datasets	Suitable for small datasets

Conclusion

Lazy evaluation is a powerful paradigm for optimizing performance and managing large datasets in JavaScript. By deferring computations and only processing data when needed, developers can build more efficient and scalable applications. With tools like generators and libraries such as Lazy.js and Lodash, JavaScript offers robust support for implementing lazy evaluation techniques.

6.4 Managing State with Functional Paradigms

State management is a critical aspect of software development, ensuring that an application behaves predictably and responds to changes effectively. In functional programming, state is managed using immutable data structures, pure functions, and declarative logic to enhance predictability and maintainability. Functional paradigms prioritize immutability and avoid shared, mutable state, which reduces bugs and makes code easier to test.

Key Principles of Functional State Management

Immutability

State is never modified directly. Instead, new copies of the state are created when changes are required.

Pure Functions

Functions that operate on state should be pure, meaning their output depends solely on their input and they produce no side effects.

Declarative Logic

State transformations are expressed declaratively, focusing on what needs to be done rather than how to do it.

Stateless Functions

Functional paradigms rely on stateless functions that calculate new states based on the current state and action.

Techniques for Managing State

1. Using Reducers

Reducers are pure functions that take the current state and an action as arguments and return a new state. They are foundational in libraries like Redux.

Example:

```javascript
Copy code
const initialState = { count: 0 };

function counterReducer(state = initialState, action) {
  switch (action.type) {
    case 'INCREMENT':
```

```javascript
    return { count: state.count + 1 };
  case 'DECREMENT':
    return { count: state.count - 1 };
  default:
    return state;
  }
}


const currentState = { count: 5 };
const newState = counterReducer(currentState, { type:
'INCREMENT' });
console.log(newState); // { count: 6 }
```

2. Immutable Data Structures

Immutability ensures that state updates do not alter existing objects but instead create new ones. Libraries like Immutable.js or native JavaScript methods (e.g., Object.assign or spread syntax) are often used.

Example:

javascript
Copy code
```javascript
const state = { count: 0 };
```

// Using spread operator for immutability
const newState = { ...state, count: state.count + 1 };
console.log(newState); // { count: 1 }
console.log(state);   // { count: 0 } (unchanged)

3. Functional Composition

State updates can be managed by composing small functions that perform specific transformations.

Example:

javascript
Copy code
```javascript
const increment = (state) => ({ ...state, count: state.count + 1 });
const double = (state) => ({ ...state, count: state.count * 2 });

const updateState = (state) => [increment, double].reduce((s, fn) => fn(s), state);

const initialState = { count: 1 };
console.log(updateState(initialState)); // { count: 4 }
```

4. Currying for State Updates

Currying allows creating specialized state update functions by pre-configuring certain arguments.

Example:

javascript

Copy code

```javascript
const updateCount = (operation) => (state) => ({
...state, count: operation(state.count) });

const increment = updateCount((count) => count + 1);
const decrement = updateCount((count) => count - 1);

const state = { count: 5 };
console.log(increment(state)); // { count: 6 }
console.log(decrement(state)); // { count: 4 }
```

5. Observables and Streams

Functional reactive programming (FRP) with tools like RxJS manages state changes over time through observable streams.

Example:

javascript
Copy code

```javascript
const { BehaviorSubject } = require('rxjs');

const state$ = new BehaviorSubject({ count: 0 });

state$.subscribe((state) => console.log('State:', state));

state$.next({ count: 1 });
state$.next({ count: 2 });
```

6. Persistent State Management

Persistent state ensures that updates are stored efficiently without altering the original structure. Libraries like Immer simplify this process.

Example with Immer:

```javascript
Copy code
const produce = require('immer');

const state = { count: 0 };

const newState = produce(state, (draft) => {
  draft.count += 1;
});

console.log(state);    // { count: 0 }
console.log(newState); // { count: 1 }
```

Benefits of Functional State Management

Predictability: Pure functions and immutability ensure that the state behaves predictably.

Debugging: Easier to debug since state transitions are explicit and trackable.

Concurrency: Avoids race conditions by preventing direct mutation of shared state.

Testability: Pure functions are easy to test in isolation.

Modularity: State logic can be broken into reusable, composable functions.

Real-World Applications

1. Frontend Frameworks

React's useReducer and useState hooks encourage functional state management.
Redux relies on reducers, immutability, and functional patterns to manage global state.

2. Backend Systems

Immutable data and pure functions simplify state transitions in server-side applications, ensuring consistency.

3. State Synchronization

Tools like RxJS manage state changes across systems, synchronizing real-time updates in a functional manner.

Conclusion

Managing state with functional paradigms provides a clean, predictable, and scalable approach to application development. By emphasizing immutability, pure functions, and declarative logic, developers can build maintainable systems that are robust against bugs and race conditions. These principles are particularly valuable in modern applications where state management is critical for performance and reliability.

Chapter 7
Performance Optimization

Performance optimization involves improving the efficiency and speed of a JavaScript application to ensure smooth user experiences and optimal resource utilization. Modern JavaScript techniques and tools enable developers to write clean, efficient code and manage performance bottlenecks effectively.

Key Strategies for Performance Optimization

Minimize DOM Manipulation

Excessive DOM interactions can slow down applications. Use virtual DOM techniques (e.g., React) or batch updates to improve performance.

Debouncing and Throttling

Limit the frequency of expensive operations, such as scroll or resize event handlers, using debouncing or throttling techniques.

Example:

```javascript
Copy code
const debounce = (func, delay) => {
  let timer;
  return (...args) => {
    clearTimeout(timer);
    timer = setTimeout(() => func(...args), delay);
  };
};
```

Code Splitting

Divide large JavaScript bundles into smaller chunks using tools like Webpack or Vite to load only necessary parts of the code.

Use Efficient Loops

Optimize loops with modern methods like map(), filter(), and reduce() instead of traditional for loops when working with arrays.

Lazy Loading

Load resources such as images, components, or data only when needed to reduce the initial page load time.

Optimize Images and Assets

Use compressed images, SVGs, or next-gen formats (like WebP). Tools like ImageMagick or online compressors can help.

Reduce Memory Usage

Avoid memory leaks by properly managing variables and cleaning up event listeners or intervals.

Use Web Workers

Offload heavy computations to background threads to prevent blocking the main thread.

Efficient State Management

Use immutable data structures and memoization to minimize unnecessary re-renders in frontend frameworks.

Minify and Compress Files

Minify JavaScript, CSS, and HTML and enable gzip or Brotli compression for faster file delivery.

Tools for Performance Optimization

Chrome DevTools: Analyze runtime performance and detect bottlenecks.
Lighthouse: Audit page performance and provide optimization suggestions.
Webpack: Implement code splitting and bundle optimization.

RxJS: Handle asynchronous operations efficiently with observables.

Conclusion

Performance optimization ensures better user experiences and resource efficiency. By leveraging modern JavaScript techniques, tools, and best practices, developers can build applications that are fast, scalable, and maintainable.

7.1 Functional Programming and Performance Trade-Offs

Functional programming (FP) offers a declarative approach to writing clean, modular, and maintainable code. However, like any paradigm, it comes with performance trade-offs. While FP can improve code quality and developer productivity, some of its inherent features may impact runtime performance or resource usage in specific scenarios. Understanding these trade-offs helps developers make informed decisions when adopting FP.

Advantages of Functional Programming for Performance

Immutability

Benefit: Immutable data structures prevent unintended side effects, making state management predictable and reducing debugging time.

Performance Note: Although copying data can be resource-intensive, optimized libraries like Immutable.js and structural sharing techniques mitigate this cost.

Pure Functions

Benefit: Pure functions are easy to test, debug, and parallelize, as they do not depend on or alter external state.

Performance Note: The absence of side effects ensures better performance in distributed systems or environments requiring concurrency.

Lazy Evaluation

Benefit: Lazy evaluation defers computations until they are needed, optimizing resource usage and handling infinite datasets.

Performance Note: It reduces unnecessary calculations, especially in large data processing tasks.
Memoization and Caching

Benefit: Pure functions enable memoization, where function results are cached for specific inputs, improving efficiency.
Performance Note: Reduces redundant calculations in applications with repetitive computations.

Performance Challenges of Functional Programming

Overhead of Immutability

Challenge: Creating new copies of data instead of modifying it in place can lead to increased memory usage and slower performance for large datasets.

Mitigation: Use libraries like Immer or Immutable.js to implement structural sharing and avoid deep copying.

Abstraction Layers

Challenge: FP often involves chaining operations (map, filter, reduce), which can introduce additional function calls and stack usage, impacting performance in tight loops or large datasets.

Mitigation: Optimize critical paths by combining operations or using transducers to minimize intermediate steps.

Recursive Operations

Challenge: FP favors recursion over loops, which can lead to stack overflow errors or slower execution compared to iterative approaches.

Mitigation: Tail call optimization (TCO) or converting recursive algorithms to iterative equivalents can address this issue.

Garbage Collection Pressure

Challenge: Frequent creation of new objects for immutability or temporary data structures in chained operations increases garbage collection workload.

Mitigation: Use efficient memory management techniques and minimize unnecessary object creation.

Learning Curve and Complexity

Challenge: Adopting FP can involve a steep learning curve, leading to less optimal code when developers are not familiar with FP techniques.

Mitigation: Provide proper training and use tools that simplify FP concepts (e.g., Ramda, Lodash).

Balancing Trade-Offs in Functional Programming

1. Hybrid Approach

Combine FP with imperative programming for performance-critical sections, using FP principles where they add the most value (e.g., immutability in state management, pure functions for logic).

2. Optimized Libraries

Use libraries like Ramda, Immutable.js, or Lodash that are designed for functional paradigms and optimized for performance.

3. Profile and Optimize

Measure performance using tools like Chrome DevTools, Lighthouse, or Node.js Performance Hooks to identify bottlenecks and optimize accordingly.

4. Avoid Over-Engineering

While FP encourages abstraction, over-abstraction can lead to unnecessary complexity and performance overhead. Focus on practical solutions.

When to Prioritize Performance over Functional Principles

Real-Time Systems

For applications with strict performance requirements (e.g., games, high-frequency trading systems), imperative approaches may be more suitable for critical paths.

Large-Scale Data Processing

In scenarios where large datasets need to be processed quickly, hybrid approaches with optimized algorithms can mitigate FP overhead.

Embedded Systems

Memory and CPU constraints in embedded systems may favor imperative, low-level programming over FP abstractions.

Conclusion

Functional programming strikes a balance between code maintainability and performance. While features like immutability and recursion may introduce overhead, the benefits in terms of reliability and scalability often outweigh these costs for most applications. By adopting hybrid approaches, leveraging optimized libraries, and profiling critical paths, developers can effectively manage the trade-offs between functional programming and performance.

7.2 Memoization

Memoization is an optimization technique used to speed up function execution by storing the results of expensive function calls and reusing them when the same inputs occur. It is particularly beneficial in functional programming, where functions are often pure and deterministic, making them suitable for caching.

How Memoization Works

Input-Output Mapping: A memoized function keeps a cache (usually an object or map) of input arguments and their corresponding outputs.

Cache Check: Before computing the result, the function checks if the result for the given inputs is already in the cache.

.

Reuse or Compute: If the result exists in the cache, it is returned immediately. Otherwise, the function computes the result, stores it in the cache, and then returns it.

Example of Memoization

Simple Example

javascript
Copy code
```javascript
function memoize(fn) {
  const cache = new Map();
  return function (...args) {
    const key = JSON.stringify(args);
    if (cache.has(key)) {
      console.log("Fetching from cache:", key);
      return cache.get(key);
    }
    console.log("Calculating result:", key);
    const result = fn(...args);
    cache.set(key, result);
    return result;
  };
}
```

```
// Expensive computation
const factorial = memoize((n) => {
  if (n === 0) return 1;
  return n * factorial(n - 1);
});

console.log(factorial(5)); // Calculates and caches
console.log(factorial(5)); // Fetches from cache
```

Benefits of Memoization

Performance Improvement

Reduces the time complexity of expensive computations by avoiding redundant calculations.

Reusability

Results for previously computed inputs are readily available.

Optimized Recursive Functions

Recursive functions like Fibonacci or factorial benefit significantly from memoization.

When to Use Memoization

Deterministic Functions

Memoization works best with pure functions, where the output depends only on the inputs and has no side effects.

Expensive Computations

Functions with heavy processing or I/O operations benefit most.

Repetitive Calls

When a function is called repeatedly with the same inputs during execution.

Example: Fibonacci with Memoization

Calculating Fibonacci numbers recursively without memoization has exponential time complexity. Memoization optimizes it to linear time.

Without Memoization

javascript
Copy code

```javascript
function fibonacci(n) {
  if (n <= 1) return n;
  return fibonacci(n - 1) + fibonacci(n - 2);
}

console.log(fibonacci(40)); // Slow due to redundant calculations
```

With Memoization

javascript
Copy code

```javascript
const memoizedFibonacci = memoize((n) => {
  if (n <= 1) return n;
  return memoizedFibonacci(n - 1) + memoizedFibonacci(n - 2);
});

console.log(memoizedFibonacci(40)); // Much faster
```

Libraries for Memoization

Lodash

Lodash provides a _.mcmoize function for memoization.

Example:

```javascript
Copy code
const _ = require('lodash');

const memoizedAdd = _.memoize((a, b) => a + b);
console.log(memoizedAdd(1, 2)); // Computes and caches
console.log(memoizedAdd(1, 2)); // Fetches from cache
```

Fast-Memoize

A lightweight and highly performant library for memoization.

Memoizee

A flexible library supporting advanced features like custom caching strategies.

Limitations of Memoization

Memory Usage

Large or unlimited caches can consume significant memory, especially for high-input variety functions.

Non-Pure Functions

Memoization is ineffective for functions with side effects or non-deterministic outputs.

Cache Management

Managing and invalidating caches for dynamic inputs can add complexity.

Overhead

For lightweight functions, memoization may introduce unnecessary overhead.

Advanced Techniques

Custom Cache Strategies

Use weak maps or LRU (Least Recently Used) caches for better memory management.

javascript
Copy code
const lruCache = new Map();
// Implement an LRU cache eviction strategy

Parameterized Memoization

Adapt memoization for multi-parameter or dynamic use cases with custom key generators.

Conclusion

Memoization is a powerful tool for optimizing JavaScript applications, especially when dealing with repetitive and expensive computations. By leveraging libraries or implementing custom solutions, developers can significantly enhance performance while maintaining functional integrity. However, careful consideration of cache size, memory usage, and applicability is crucial to maximize its benefits.

7.3 Throttling and Debouncing

Throttling and debouncing are performance optimization techniques that regulate the frequency of function execution in response to events like scrolling, resizing, or typing. These techniques are essential for improving application performance, particularly when handling high-frequency events.

Throttling

Throttling ensures a function is executed at most once within a specified time interval, regardless of how many times the event is triggered. This is useful when you want to limit the frequency of function execution.

Use Cases

Limiting API calls during continuous input events.
Handling window resizing or scrolling events.
Tracking mouse movements.

Implementation Example

javascript
Copy code

```javascript
function throttle(func, delay) {
  let lastCall = 0;
  return function (...args) {
    const now = Date.now();
    if (now - lastCall >= delay) {
      lastCall = now;
      func(...args);
    }
  };
}

// Usage
const handleScroll = throttle(() => {
  console.log("Throttled Scroll Event");
}, 1000);

window.addEventListener("scroll", handleScroll);
```

Debouncing

Debouncing ensures that a function is executed only after a specified delay since the last time the event was triggered. This is useful for delaying execution until the event has stopped firing.

Use Cases

Delaying search query execution in a search bar until the user stops typing.
Avoiding excessive validation checks on form input fields.
Optimizing resize or scroll events.

Implementation Example

javascript
Copy code
```
function debounce(func, delay) {
  let timer;
  return function (...args) {
    clearTimeout(timer);
    timer = setTimeout(() => func(...args), delay);
  };
}

// Usage
```

```
const handleInput = debounce((event) => {
        console.log("Debounced    Input      Event:",
event.target.value);
}, 500);

document.getElementById("inputField").addEventListener(
"input", handleInput);
```

Differences Between Throttling and Debouncing

Aspect	Throttling	Debouncing
Execution Timing	Executes the function at regular intervals.	Executes the function after the event stops.
Use Case	Regulating repeated events over time	Executing after a pause in events.

Example	· Tracking scroll position every second	Triggering a search after typing stops.

·

Key Libraries for Throttling and Debouncing

Lodash

Provides built-in methods for throttling and debouncing.

Example:

```javascript
Copy code
const _ = require("lodash");

const throttledFn = _.throttle(() => console.log("Throttled"), 1000);
const debouncedFn = _.debounce(() => console.log("Debounced"), 500);
```

```
window.addEventListener("scroll", throttledFn);
document.getElementById("inputField").addEventListener(
"input", debouncedFn);
```

RxJS

Reactive extensions for JavaScript include operators like throttleTime and debounceTime for handling events in streams.

When to Use

Throttling: Use when you need to perform actions at consistent intervals, such as tracking scroll progress or limiting API calls.
Debouncing: Use when you need to wait until a burst of events has stopped, such as processing search input or resizing windows.

Conclusion

Throttling and debouncing are indispensable tools for optimizing event handling in JavaScript applications. By regulating function execution, these techniques help reduce unnecessary computations, improve performance, and enhance user experience. Selecting the right technique depends on the use case and the desired execution pattern.

Chapter 8
Real-World Applications

Throttling and debouncing are widely used in real-world web applications to enhance performance and improve user experience. Below are some practical applications:

1. Search Input Optimization (Debouncing)

Scenario: In search bars or autocomplete features, executing an API call after every keystroke can overload the server. Solution: Use debouncing to wait until the user finishes typing before sending a request.

Example:

```javascript
Copy code
const searchHandler = debounce((query) => fetchResults(query), 500);
inputField.addEventListener("input", (e) => searchHandler(e.target.value));
```

2. Scroll Event Optimization (Throttling)

Scenario: Scroll events trigger frequently, potentially leading to performance issues in tasks like updating progress indicators or loading content.

Solution: Use throttling to execute these actions at fixed intervals.

Example:

javascript
Copy code
const updateProgress = throttle(() => updateScrollProgress(), 200); window.addEventListener("scroll", updateProgress);

3. Window Resize Handling (Debouncing)

Scenario: Handling resizing events can trigger layout recalculations and reflows.
Solution: Use debouncing to update layout or UI elements only after the resizing has stopped.

Example:

javascript
Copy code
const resizeHandler = debounce(() => adjustLayout(), 300);

window.addEventListener("resize", resizeHandler);

4. Rate Limiting API Calls (Throttling)

Scenario: Limiting the frequency of API calls in features like infinite scrolling or live data fetching.
Solution: Use throttling to control the rate of requests.

Example:

```javascript
Copy code
const fetchMoreData = throttle(() =>
loadMoreContent(), 1000);
window.addEventListener("scroll", fetchMoreData);
```

5. Form Validation (Debouncing)

Scenario: Validating form fields in real-time can cause excessive processing.
Solution: Use debouncing to validate only after the user stops typing.

Example:

```javascript
Copy code
const validateInput = debounce((input) =>
checkValidity(input), 300);
inputField.addEventListener("input", (e) =>
validateInput(e.target.value));
```

6. Mouse Move Tracking (Throttling)

Scenario: Tracking mouse movements to update tooltips or animations can be resource-intensive.

Solution: Use throttling to update positions or perform calculations at fixed intervals.

Example:

```javascript
Copy code
const trackMouse = throttle((e) =>
updateTooltip(e.clientX, e.clientY), 50);
window.addEventListener("mousemove", trackMouse);
```

Conclusion

Throttling and debouncing are essential techniques for managing high-frequency events in modern web development. They help maintain application performance while ensuring responsive and efficient user interactions.

8.1 Functional Patterns in React and Redux

React and Redux are popular tools in modern frontend development, and they strongly encourage functional programming principles. By applying functional patterns, developers can create maintainable, predictable, and reusable components and state management systems.

1. Stateless Functional Components

React encourages the use of stateless functional components, which are simple functions that take props as arguments and return JSX. They are easy to test, understand, and compose.

Example:

javascript
Copy code
```
const Greeting = ({ name }) => <h1>Hello, {name}!</h1>;
```

Benefits:

Simplified syntax and better readability.
No lifecycle methods or state, which makes them pure and predictable.
Improved performance through optimizations like React.memo.

2. Pure Functions and Immutability

Both React and Redux benefit from pure functions and immutability to ensure predictable state changes.

React Example:

```javascript
Copy code
const addItem = (items, newItem) => [...items, newItem];
```

Redux Example (Reducer):

```javascript
Copy code
const todosReducer = (state = [], action) => {
  switch (action.type) {
    case "ADD_TODO":
      return [...state, { text: action.payload, completed: false }];
    default:
      return state;
  }
};
```

Benefits:

Predictable state transitions.
Easier debugging with tools like Redux DevTools.

Enables time travel debugging.

3. Higher-Order Components (HOCs)

Higher-order components are functions that take a component and return a new enhanced component. They promote reusability and composability.

Example:

javascript
Copy code

```javascript
const withLoading = (Component) => ({ isLoading, ...props }) => {
  return isLoading ? <p>Loading...</p> : <Component {...props} />;
};

const DataComponent = withLoading(({ data }) => <div>{data}</div>);
```

Benefits:

Encapsulate shared logic.
Promote code reuse and separation of concerns.

4. Hooks: Functional State and Effects

Hooks in React allow developers to use state and lifecycle features in functional components, further embracing functional programming.

Common Hooks:

useState: Manage state.
useEffect: Handle side effects.
useReducer: Use reducer patterns in functional components.
useMemo and useCallback: Optimize performance.

Example:
Javascript
Copy code
```
const Counter = () => {
  const [count, setCount] = useState(0);

  return (
   <div>
    <p>Count: {count}</p>
```

```
       <button  onClick={()  =>  setCount(count  +
1)}>Increment</button>
  </div>
 );
};
```

5. Functional Composition

React's declarative nature promotes composing components
together to build more complex UIs.

Example:
javascript
Copy code
```
const Header = () => <header>Header</header>;
const Footer = () => <footer>Footer</footer>;

const Page = () => (
  <div>
    <Header />
    <main>Content goes here</main>
    <Footer />
  </div>
);
```

Benefits:

Modular and reusable components.
Clean and maintainable code.

6. Redux Selectors and Memoization

Selectors are functions that derive data from the Redux store. Memoized selectors using libraries like Reselect avoid unnecessary recalculations, improving performance.

Example:

javascript
Copy code
```
import { createSelector } from "reselect";

const selectTodos = (state) => state.todos;
const selectCompletedTodos = createSelector(
  [selectTodos],
  (todos) => todos.filter((todo) => todo.completed)
);
```

7. Middleware for Functional Side Effects

Redux middleware allows functional handling of side effects such as API calls, logging, or analytics.

Example with Redux Thunk:

javascript
Copy code

```
const fetchTodos = () => async (dispatch) => {
  const response = await fetch("/api/todos");
  const data = await response.json();
  dispatch({ type: "SET_TODOS", payload: data });
};
```

8. Immutability with Libraries

Libraries like Immer or Immutable.js help enforce immutability in Redux reducers and state updates.

Example with Immer:

javascript
Copy code

```
import produce from "immer";

const todosReducer = (state = [], action) =>
```

```
produce(state, (draft) => {
  switch (action.type) {
  case "ADD_TODO":
    draft.push({ text: action.payload, completed: false
});
    break;
  default:
    break;
  }
});
```

Benefits of Functional Patterns in React and Redux

Predictability: Pure functions and immutability make state management predictable and easier to debug.

Reusability: Functional components and HOCs promote modularity and reuse.

Performance: Memoization and optimized hooks reduce unnecessary re-renders.

Scalability: Functional patterns help manage complex UIs and state logic effectively.

Maintainability: Clean and declarative code improves readability and reduces technical debt.

Conclusion

Functional patterns in React and Redux enhance code quality, performance, and maintainability by embracing principles like immutability, pure functions, and composition. By leveraging features such as hooks, reducers, HOCs, and middleware, developers can build scalable and efficient applications while adhering to functional programming paradigms.

8.2 Handling Asynchronous Data Streams with RxJS

RxJS (Reactive Extensions for JavaScript) is a library for working with asynchronous and event-based data streams using observable sequences. It provides powerful tools to handle complex data flows, making it easier to manage asynchronous operations like API calls, user interactions, or real-time updates in a declarative way.

Core Concepts in RxJS

Observable

Represents a data stream that can emit values over time (e.g., numbers, objects, events).

Observer

A set of callbacks (next, error, complete) that listen to an observable's emitted values.

Subscription

The process of connecting an observer to an observable to start receiving data.

Operators

Functions used to transform, filter, or combine data streams (e.g., map, filter, merge).

Subjects

A special type of observable that acts as both an observable and an observer, allowing multicasting.

Key Features of RxJS

Declarative Syntax

RxJS allows developers to declare how data flows through streams using composable operators.

Time Management

Supports time-based operations like throttling, debouncing, and buffering.

Asynchronous Handling

Simplifies managing multiple asynchronous events with a unified API.

Working with RxJS: Basic Example

Observable and Subscription

javascript
Copy code
```javascript
import { Observable } from "rxjs";
```

```javascript
// Create an observable
const observable = new Observable((subscriber) => {
  subscriber.next("Hello");
  subscriber.next("World");
  subscriber.complete();
});

// Subscribe to the observable
observable.subscribe({
  next: (value) => console.log(value),
  complete: () => console.log("Stream complete!"),
});
```

Output:

arduino

Copy code

Hello

World

Stream complete!

Real-World Use Cases

Handling User Input RxJS can debounce or throttle user input, such as in search fields.

javascript

Copy code
```javascript
import { fromEvent } from "rxjs";
import { debounceTime, map } from "rxjs/operators";

const input = document.getElementById("search");
const input$ = fromEvent(input, "input");

input$
  .pipe(
    debounceTime(300),
    map((event) => event.target.value)
  )
  .subscribe((value) => console.log(`Search: ${value}`));
```

Real-Time Updates RxJS is ideal for handling WebSocket or server-sent events.

javascript
Copy code
```javascript
import { webSocket } from "rxjs/webSocket";

const socket$ = webSocket("ws://example.com/socket");
socket$.subscribe((data) => console.log(data));
```
API Calls Combine multiple API calls and handle them sequentially or in parallel.

```javascript
Copy code
import { ajax } from "rxjs/ajax";
import { forkJoin } from "rxjs";

const user$ = ajax.getJSON("/api/user");
const posts$ = ajax.getJSON("/api/posts");

forkJoin([user$, posts$]).subscribe(([user, posts]) => {
  console.log("User:", user);
  console.log("Posts:", posts);
});
```

Popular RxJS Operators

Transformation

map: Transform emitted values.

switchMap: Map to an inner observable and switch to its emissions.

mergeMap: Map to an inner observable and merge all outputs.

Filtering

filter: Emit values that satisfy a condition.

debounceTime: Emit values after a specified time of silence.

take: Take the first n emissions.

Combination

merge: Combine multiple observables concurrently.

concat: Combine observables sequentially.

combineLatest: Emit when any input observable emits.

Error Handling

catchError: Handle errors in a stream.

retry: Retry the observable on error.

Advanced Example: Search with API Integration
Scenario

Implement a search input field that queries an API with debounced user input.

Implementation

javascript

```
Copy code
import { fromEvent } from "rxjs";
import { debounceTime, distinctUntilChanged,
switchMap, catchError } from "rxjs/operators";
import { ajax } from "rxjs/ajax";

const input = document.getElementById("search");
const search$ = fromEvent(input, "input");

search$
 .pipe(
   debounceTime(300),
   distinctUntilChanged(),
   switchMap((event) =>

ajax.getJSON(`/api/search?q=${event.target.value}`).pip
e(
     catchError((error) => {
       console.error("Error:", error);
       return [];
     })
   )
  )
 )
```

```
.subscribe((results)    =>    console.log("Results:",
results));
```

Benefits of Using RxJS

Simplified Asynchronous Logic
Makes complex asynchronous workflows easier to understand and maintain.

Powerful Data Stream Management

Handles streams of events, data, and time with a consistent API.

Efficient Resource Usage

Optimizes performance by reducing redundant operations (e.g., debouncing user input).

Improved Code Readability

Declarative patterns make it easier to follow how data flows through the application.

Challenges of RxJS

Learning Curve

The concepts of observables and operators can be difficult for beginners.

Overhead

Using RxJS for simple tasks can introduce unnecessary complexity.

Debugging

Debugging long, operator-heavy pipelines can be challenging.

Conclusion

RxJS is a powerful library for handling asynchronous data streams in JavaScript applications. By leveraging its observables, operators, and subjects, developers can create robust solutions for user interactions, real-time data, and complex workflows. While it has a learning curve, RxJS's benefits in simplifying and optimizing asynchronous logic make it a valuable tool for modern web development.

8.3 Functional Programming in Back-End JavaScript (Node.js)

Functional programming (FP) is a programming paradigm centered around using pure functions, immutability, and declarative patterns to build applications. Node.js, being a JavaScript runtime, supports FP principles and patterns, making it possible to write clean, maintainable, and efficient back-end applications.

Why Use Functional Programming in Node.js?

Modularity: Functions can be reused across different parts of the application, reducing duplication.

Immutability: Prevents unintended side effects, leading to more predictable code.

Asynchronous Handling: FP complements Node.js's event-driven, asynchronous nature, enabling better management of asynchronous workflows.

Testability: Pure functions are easier to test and debug.
Scalability: Functional patterns are well-suited for building scalable applications, especially when handling data streams.
Core Functional Programming Concepts in Node.js

1. Pure Functions

Pure functions depend only on their input parameters and produce the same output every time, without side effects.

Example:

javascript
Copy code
```
const add = (a, b) => a + b;

console.log(add(2, 3)); // Always 5
```

2. Immutability

Immutability involves avoiding changes to existing data structures. Instead, new data structures are created when updates are needed.

Example:

```javascript
Copy code
const updateUser = (user, updates) => ({ ...user,
...updates });

const user = { name: "Alice", age: 25 };
const updatedUser = updateUser(user, { age: 26 });

console.log(updatedUser); // { name: "Alice", age: 26 }
console.log(user);      // Original remains unchanged
```

3. Higher-Order Functions

Functions that take other functions as arguments or return functions are called higher-order functions. Node.js heavily relies on this concept.

Example:

```javascript
Copy code
const logger = (level) => (message) =>
console.log(`[${level}] ${message}`);
```

```javascript
const infoLogger = logger("INFO");
infoLogger("Server started"); // [INFO] Server started
```

4. Asynchronous Functional Patterns

Node.js provides native support for handling asynchronous operations, often using promises and async/await in functional styles.

Example:

javascript
Copy code
```javascript
const fetchData = async (url) => {
  const response = await fetch(url);
  const data = await response.json();
  return data;
};
```

Functional Programming Techniques in Node.js

1. Composing Middleware

Middleware functions in frameworks like Express.js are composable, reflecting FP principles.

Example:

```javascript
Copy code
const logger = (req, res, next) => {
  console.log(`${req.method} ${req.url}`);
  next();
};

const validate = (req, res, next) => {
  if (!req.body.name) {
    res.status(400).send("Name is required");
  } else {
    next();
  }
};

app.use(logger);
app.post("/users", validate, (req, res) => {
  res.send("User created");
});
```

2. Data Transformation with Streams

Node.js streams are inherently functional, allowing transformations with methods like .pipe().

Example:

```javascript
Copy code
const fs = require("fs");
const zlib = require("zlib");

fs.createReadStream("input.txt")
  .pipe(zlib.createGzip())
  .pipe(fs.createWriteStream("output.txt.gz"));
```

3. Declarative Routing

Libraries like Express or Fastify enable declarative route definitions.

Example:

```javascript
Copy code
```

```javascript
app.get("/users", async (req, res) => {
  const users = await getUsers();
  res.json(users);
});
```

4. Functional Error Handling

Using functional patterns to handle errors improves code readability and reduces nested structures.

Example:

```javascript
Copy code
const tryCatch = (fn) => async (req, res, next) => {
  try {
    await fn(req, res);
  } catch (error) {
    next(error);
  }
};

app.get("/data", tryCatch(async (req, res) => {
  const data = await fetchData();
  res.json(data);
```

}));

Libraries for Functional Programming in Node.js

Ramda: A utility library for functional programming with a focus on immutability and composition.

Example:

```javascript
Copy code
const R = require("ramda");

const double = (x) => x * 2;
const increment = (x) => x + 1;
const process = R.pipe(increment, double);

console.log(process(3)); // 8
```

Lodash/fp: A functional programming version of Lodash.

Example:

```javascript
Copy code
```

```
const _ = require("lodash/fp");

const data = [1, 2, 3, 4];
const result = _.flow(
  _.map((x) => x * 2),
  _.filter((x) => x > 4)
)(data);

console.log(result); // [6, 8]
```

RxJS: Ideal for managing asynchronous data streams and event handling.

Advantages of Functional Programming in Node.js

Better Code Readability: Declarative patterns make code easier to understand.

Reusability: Modular, pure functions reduce duplication. Improved Testability: Functions without side effects are easier to test.

Scalability: Functional paradigms scale well in large applications, especially when handling streams or complex data flows.

Challenges

Learning Curve: FP requires a shift in thinking, especially for developers used to imperative styles.
Performance Overhead: Excessive use of immutable structures or pure functions may impact performance in some scenarios.
Debugging: Functional chains can be harder to debug compared to imperative code.

Conclusion

Functional programming in Node.js promotes cleaner, modular, and more predictable code, making it suitable for modern back-end development. By leveraging concepts like pure functions, immutability, and higher-order functions, and combining them with powerful libraries, developers can build scalable and maintainable applications. While there are challenges, the benefits of functional patterns often outweigh the complexities, especially for applications requiring high scalability and maintainability.

Chapter 9
Best Practices and Tips

Adopting functional programming (FP) in JavaScript can lead to cleaner, maintainable, and more predictable code. Here are some best practices and tips to help you make the most of FP principles:

1. Use Pure Functions

Ensure functions depend only on input parameters and have no side effects.
Benefits: Predictability, testability, and ease of debugging.

Example:

```javascript
const square = (x) => x * x;
console.log(square(4)); // Always 16
```

2. Embrace Immutability

Avoid modifying existing objects or arrays; instead, return new ones.
Use tools like Object.freeze(), the spread operator, or libraries like Immer.

Example:

javascript
Copy code
const addItem = (arr, item) => [...arr, item];

3. Leverage Higher-Order Functions

Use functions like map(), filter(), and reduce() to handle transformations declaratively.
Example:

javascript
Copy code
const numbers = [1, 2, 3];
const doubled = numbers.map((x) => x * 2); // [2, 4, 6]

4. Use Composition Over Nesting

Combine functions using tools like pipe() or compose() for better readability and reusability.
Example (using a custom compose):

javascript
Copy code
```
const compose = (...fns) => (x) => fns.reduceRight((y, f) => f(y), x);

const double = (x) => x * 2;
const increment = (x) => x + 1;

const process = compose(double, increment);
console.log(process(3)); // 8
```

5. Minimize Side Effects

Isolate side effects (e.g., API calls, logging) in specific functions and keep them separate from core logic.
Example:

javascript
Copy code

```javascript
const fetchData = async (url) => fetch(url).then((res) => res.json());
```

6. Favor Declarative Code

Write code that describes what it does, not how it does it.
Imperative:

javascript
Copy code

```javascript
let sum = 0;
for (let i = 0; i < numbers.length; i++) {
  sum += numbers[i];
}
```

Declarative:

javascript
Copy code

```javascript
const sum = numbers.reduce((acc, val) => acc + val, 0);
```

7. Use Libraries for Complex Tasks

Libraries like Ramda, Lodash/fp, and RxJS simplify FP concepts like currying, composition, and asynchronous data streams.

8. Write Small, Composable Functions

Break down logic into small, reusable functions that perform single tasks.

Example:

javascript
Copy code
```javascript
const isEven = (x) => x % 2 === 0;
const square = (x) => x * x;

const processNumbers = (arr) => arr.filter(isEven).map(square);
```

9. Avoid Mutating Shared State
Always clone and update state instead of mutating shared objects or arrays.

10. Learn and Apply Recursion

Replace loops with recursion for tasks like traversing trees or performing repeated calculations.

11. Optimize with Memoization

Use memoization to cache expensive function results and avoid redundant computations.
Example:

javascript
Copy code

```javascript
const memoize = (fn) => {
  const cache = {};
  return (arg) => {
    if (cache[arg]) return cache[arg];
    return (cache[arg] – fn(arg));
  };
};
```

12. Test and Debug Functional Code

Write tests for individual pure functions to ensure correctness.

Use tools like Jest for testing and Redux DevTools for debugging state management.

Conclusion

By adhering to these best practices, you can unlock the full potential of functional programming in JavaScript. Start small, integrate FP principles gradually, and leverage tools and libraries to make your code more robust, maintainable, and scalable.

9.1 Balancing Functional and Imperative Code

While functional programming (FP) offers many benefits, it is not always practical or efficient to adopt it exclusively. Combining functional and imperative programming allows developers to strike a balance between readability, performance, and maintainability in JavaScript applications.

Key Considerations for Balancing Functional and Imperative Code

Readability Over Purity

While functional code is often cleaner and more predictable, overly abstract FP techniques can make code harder to understand. Use functional patterns where they enhance clarity but switch to imperative code when it simplifies the logic.

Example (Readable Imperative Code):

```javascript
Copy code
let total = 0;
for (let i = 0; i < numbers.length; i++) {
  total += numbers[i];
}
```

Example (Functional Equivalent):

```javascript
Copy code
```

```javascript
const total = numbers.reduce((acc, num) => acc + num,
0);
```

Performance

Functional programming emphasizes immutability and pure functions, which can lead to performance overhead, especially with large datasets or deep recursion. Use imperative code for performance-critical sections, like loops, when necessary.

Example (Loop for Efficiency):

```javascript
Copy code
let sum = 0;
for (const num of numbers) {
  sum += num;
}
```

When to Use Functional Programming

Data Transformation

Functional programming excels in transforming and processing data streams or collections. Use functions like map(), filter(), and reduce() for concise and declarative transformations.

Example:

javascript
Copy code
```
const evenNumbers = numbers.filter((n) => n % 2 === 0).map((n) => n * 2);
```

Immutability Requirements

Use FP for scenarios requiring immutability, such as managing state in applications like React or Redux.

Example:

javascript
Copy code
```
const updatedState = { ...state, count: state.count + 1 };
```

Reusable Logic

When logic is reused in multiple places, FP patterns like higher-order functions and composition make the code modular and maintainable.

Example:

javascript
Copy code
```javascript
const double = (x) => x * 2;
const increment = (x) => x + 1;

const process = (x) => double(increment(x));
```

When to Use Imperative Programming

Simple Logic

For straightforward, step-by-step operations, imperative code is often easier to write and understand.

Example:

javascript
Copy code
```javascript
const results = [];
```

```
for (const item of items) {
  if (item.active) results.push(item.name);
}
```

Low-Level Operations

Use imperative patterns for tasks like file handling, database transactions, or performance-critical loops.

Complex State Management

In cases where managing state with FP patterns becomes too verbose or complex, imperative code may simplify the process.

Blending Functional and Imperative Code

Hybrid Approach

Combine both paradigms within the same codebase, using functional programming for declarative logic and imperative code for performance-critical or simpler sections.

Example:

javascript
Copy code
```javascript
const processedItems = items
  .filter((item) => item.active)
      .map((item)     =>     ({    ...item,     name:
item.name.toUpperCase() }));

for (const item of processedItems) {
  console.log(item.name);
}
```

Isolate Functional Code

Encapsulate functional patterns in reusable modules or utility functions, allowing imperative code to call them as needed.

Example:

javascript
Copy code
```javascript
const filterActive = (items) => items.filter((item) =>
item.active);

const activeItems = filterActive(items);
```

```
for (const item of activeItems) {
  console.log(item.name);
}
```

Benefits of Balancing Both Approaches

Readability: Developers can choose the paradigm that best suits the task at hand, improving clarity.

Performance: Performance-critical sections can use imperative patterns without sacrificing maintainability.

Flexibility: Adopting a hybrid approach allows teams to benefit from both paradigms without being overly rigid.

Conclusion

Balancing functional and imperative programming allows you to maximize the strengths of each paradigm while minimizing their limitations. By thoughtfully choosing the right approach for each task, developers can write code that is both efficient and maintainable, leading to better software solutions.

9.2 Debugging Functional Code

Functional programming (FP) emphasizes immutability, pure functions, and declarative patterns, which often result in cleaner and more predictable code. However, debugging functional code can present unique challenges, especially for developers transitioning from imperative programming. Understanding effective debugging strategies can simplify the process and make FP more approachable.

Common Challenges in Debugging Functional Code

Function Chaining

Long chains of transformations using methods like map(), filter(), and reduce() can obscure where errors occur.

Immutability

Immutable data structures make it harder to track changes and state over time.

Higher-Order Functions

Functions returning or accepting other functions can lead to obscure stack traces.

Asynchronous Code

Debugging promises, callbacks, or streams in FP can complicate identifying issues.

Strategies for Debugging Functional Code

1. Use Descriptive Function Names

Replace anonymous functions with named functions to improve stack trace readability and make code self-documenting.

Example:

javascript
Copy code
```javascript
const double = (x) => x * 2;
const increment = (x) => x + 1;
```

```javascript
const result = [1, 2, 3].map(double).map(increment);
```

2. Break Down Chains

Split long function chains into smaller steps to identify where errors occur.

Example:

```javascript
Copy code
// Complex chain
const result = [1, 2, 3].map((x) => x * 2).filter((x) => x > 4).reduce((a, b) => a + b, 0);

// Debug-friendly
const doubled = [1, 2, 3].map((x) => x * 2);
const filtered = doubled.filter((x) => x > 4);
const sum = filtered.reduce((a, b) => a + b, 0);
```

3. Add Logging

Insert console.log statements at key points to track intermediate values in function chains.

Example:

```javascript
Copy code
const result = [1, 2, 3]
  .map((x) => {
   console.log("After map:", x);
   return x * 2;
 })
 .filter((x) => {
   console.log("After filter:", x);
   return x > 4;
 });
```

4. Debug with Pure Functions

Pure functions depend only on their inputs and outputs, making them easy to isolate and test.
Example:

```javascript
Copy code
const square = (x) => x * x;

console.log(square(4)); // Test function independently
```

5. Use Debugging Tools

Browser DevTools: Use breakpoints to pause code execution and inspect values.

Node.js Debugger: Run Node.js with --inspect to debug server-side functional code.

Redux DevTools: Debug state changes in functional React/Redux applications.

6. Leverage Functional Libraries

Libraries like Ramda and Lodash/fp often provide well-tested utilities that reduce the risk of bugs. Use their documentation to understand error scenarios.

7. Isolate Side Effects

Keep side effects (e.g., API calls, logging) separate from core logic to make debugging simpler.

Example:

```javascript
Copy code
const fetchData = async (url) => {
  console.log("Fetching data from:", url);
  const response = await fetch(url);
  return response.json();
};
```

8. Debug Recursion

Replace recursive functions with an iterative equivalent temporarily to better understand errors.
Example:

```javascript
Copy code
// Recursive
const factorial = (n) => (n === 0 ? 1 : n * factorial(n - 1));

// Debug-friendly
const factorialIterative = (n) => {
  let result = 1;
  for (let i = 1; i <= n; i++) result *= i;
  return result;
```

};

9. Use TypeScript or JSDoc

Add type annotations to catch errors like passing unexpected arguments to functional pipelines.

Example:

typescript
Copy code
const add = (a: number, b: number): number => a + b;

10. Test Incrementally

Write unit tests for individual functions before integrating them into larger chains. Tools like Jest or Mocha can help.

Example:

javascript
Copy code
```
test("square function", () => {
  expect(square(3)).toBe(9);
});
```

Debugging Asynchronous Functional Code

Inspect Promises: Use .catch() to handle and log errors in promise chains.

Example:

```javascript
Copy code
fetchData("https://api.example.com")
  .then((data) => console.log(data))
  .catch((err) => console.error("Error:", err));
```

Async/Await Debugging: Wrap async code in try-catch blocks for better error visibility.

Example:

```javascript
Copy code
try {
        const data = await fetchData("https://api.example.com");
  console.log(data);
} catch (err) {
```

```
  console.error("Error:", err);
}
```

Debug Streams: Use libraries like RxJS with operators like tap() for logging intermediate values.

Example:

```javascript
Copy code
const { from } = require("rxjs");
const { map, tap } = require("rxjs/operators");

from([1, 2, 3])
  .pipe(
    tap((x) => console.log("Before map:", x)),
    map((x) => x * 2),
    tap((x) => console.log("After map:", x))
  )
  .subscribe();
```

Best Practices

Write small, single-purpose functions to simplify debugging.

Use declarative patterns, but don't hesitate to switch to imperative styles when debugging.

Document complex functional chains for easier understanding.

Utilize logging and testing tools proactively to catch errors early.

Conclusion

Debugging functional code requires a structured approach, leveraging tools and techniques like logging, function isolation, and modular design. By following these strategies, you can effectively identify and resolve issues in functional programming, ensuring your code remains both robust and maintainable.

9.3 Writing Readable and Maintainable Code

Readable and maintainable code is the cornerstone of a successful software project. It allows developers to understand, extend, and debug code easily, ensuring long-term productivity and reducing technical debt. Here are key principles and practices for writing code that is both readable and maintainable.

Key Principles

1. Keep It Simple (KISS)

Avoid over-complicating your code with unnecessary abstractions or features.

Write straightforward solutions that are easy to understand and follow.

Example:

javascript
Copy code
```javascript
// Complex and unnecessary abstraction
const operation = (x, func) => func(x);
console.log(operation(5, (x) => x * x));
```

```javascript
// Simple and direct
const square = (x) => x * x;
console.log(square(5));
```

2. Follow Consistent Coding Conventions

Use consistent naming conventions, indentation, and formatting.
Leverage tools like Prettier or ESLint to enforce a consistent style.

Example (Camel Case):

javascript
Copy code
```javascript
const userProfile = { firstName: "John", lastName: "Doe" };
```

3. Write Self-Documenting Code
Use meaningful variable, function, and class names that describe their purpose.
Avoid cryptic or overly generic names.

Example:

javascript
Copy code
// Bad
const x = [1, 2, 3];

// Good
const numbers = [1, 2, 3];

4. Modularize Your Code

Break your code into small, reusable functions and modules to avoid duplication and improve readability.

Example:

javascript
Copy code
// Modular code
const calculateArea = (width, height) => width * height;
const calculatePerimeter = (width, height) => 2 * (width + height);

5. Write Pure Functions

Pure functions are predictable, making them easier to test and debug.
They depend only on their input parameters and do not cause side effects.

Example:

javascript
Copy code
const add = (a, b) => a + b; // Pure

6. Use Comments Judiciously

Write comments only when the code's intent is not immediately obvious.
Avoid redundant or outdated comments.

Example:

javascript
Copy code

```javascript
// Calculates the square of a number
const square = (x) => x * x; // Comment not necessary
```

7. Leverage Modern JavaScript Features

Use modern ES6+ syntax like let, const, arrow functions, destructuring, and modules to write concise and expressive code.

Example:

javascript
Copy code
```javascript
const numbers = [1, 2, 3];
const doubled = numbers.map((n) => n * 2); // Modern approach
```

8. Handle Errors Gracefully

Anticipate and handle potential errors with try-catch blocks or default cases to prevent runtime crashes.

Example:

```javascript
Copy code
try {
  const data = JSON.parse(userInput);
} catch (error) {
  console.error("Invalid JSON input:", error);
}
```

9. Avoid Hardcoding

Use constants, configuration files, or environment variables for values that might change.

Example:

```javascript
Copy code
// Hardcoded
const API_URL = "https://api.example.com";

// Use environment variables
const API_URL = process.env.API_URL;
```

10. Optimize for Performance and Readability

Strike a balance between writing performant code and keeping it readable.

Example:

javascript
Copy code
```
// Readable but less performant for large arrays
const unique = [...new Set(arr)];

// Faster for large arrays
const unique = Array.from(new Set(arr));
```

Best Practices

1. Use Consistent Folder Structures

Organize your files logically, separating concerns (e.g., components, utilities, services).

Example:

css
Copy code
src/
  components/
  utils/
  services/

2. Write Tests

Use unit tests, integration tests, and end-to-end tests to ensure code reliability.
Tools like Jest, Mocha, and Cypress are great options.

3. Refactor Regularly

Refactor code to remove redundancy, improve structure, and align with new requirements.

4. Use Tools and Libraries

Tools like ESLint, Prettier, and libraries like Lodash and Ramda can simplify development and enforce best practices.

Benefits of Readable and Maintainable Code

Easier Collaboration

Clear, well-structured code makes it easier for team members to understand and contribute.

Reduced Bugs

Maintainable code is easier to test and debug, reducing the likelihood of errors.

Faster Development

Clear code reduces the time spent deciphering logic, accelerating development.

Longevity

Well-maintained code is more adaptable to future changes.

Conclusion

Readable and maintainable code is not just about aesthetics; it's a practical investment in the quality and sustainability of your software. By following best practices like modularization, consistent conventions, and error handling, you can create code that is easy to understand, extend, and maintain, ensuring long-term project success.

www.ingramcontent.com/pod-product-compliance
Lightning Source LLC
LaVergne TN
LVHW022336060326
832902LV00022B/4062